ARCHITECTURAL CRITICISM AND JOURNALISM: GLOBAL PERSPECTIVES

Proceedings of an International Seminar organised by the
Aga Khan Award for Architecture
in association with the Kuwait Society of Engineers

6–7 December 2005, Kuwait

EDITED BY MOHAMMAD AL-ASAD WITH MAJD MUSA

UMBERTO ALLEMANDI & C.
for

Aga Khan Award for Architecture

Aga Khan Award for Architecture

CICA

Comité International des Critiques d'Architecture
International Committee of Architectural Critics
Comité Internacional de Críticos de Arquitectura

Front cover
Kuwait City on a foggy morning, photo by Kamran Adle.

Back cover
Kuwait Water Towers, recipient of the 1980
Aga Khan Award for Architecture, photo by Kamran Adle.

Foreword

SUHA ÖZKAN, CHAIRMAN, WORLD ARCHITECTURE COMMUNITY
FORMER SECRETARY GENERAL, AGA KHAN AWARD FOR ARCHITECTURE

The most important aim of the theories of arts and sciences is to guide practice and validate implementation. With the rise of positivism, scientists almost unanimously accepted the process of experimentation in order to validate what would be the 'truth', even though eminent philosophers like Sir Karl Popper (d. 1994) challenged the existence of any 'absolute truth' and preferred to use the concept of 'verisimilitude' (or truth-likeliness) for validating scientific knowledge. In contrast, the world of arts bases the validity of contributions on 'originality'. Although originality as a criterion may be very easy to define in the abstract, it is not so easy to agree on what is original and what is not.

Architecture is neither a pure art that may benefit from the theoretical premises of the arts nor a sheer applied science that may benefit from the assertions of the sciences. It uses the applied physical sciences to allow us to build safely and comfortably. Its major preoccupation, however, is to mould space and create forms. This preoccupation lends itself to the 'softer' aspects of knowledge, which are the theories of arts and the forces of the psychological and social realm.

When architectural form develops through traditional processes, the situation is different. The values that generate form, and the climatic, material and technological forces that enable builders to accomplish that form have been determined through a long historical process. Function, symbolic values, materials and technology all act together to generate form. The process of determination of validity therefore lies within the communities that create that architecture.

As architecture has become a professional activity, the mastery and creativity of the individual architect have become important. During the periods that preceded the Renaissance in the West, such as the Romanesque and the Gothic, the knowledge of architecture was maintained in the hands of the few who protected the profession. These were, as Joseph Rykwert has asserted in this volume, the guilds of masons and master-builders. It was during the Renaissance that architectural knowledge became accessible to the individual rather than belonging exclusively to the guild member, and this development obviously owes a great deal to the invention of printing.

In addition to making the rapid and widespread dissemination of documents possible, the printing press also produced the manuals that functioned as documents for valid building systems. These, of course, were mainly in line with the prevalent values of the Renaissance, which favoured the perpetuation of the Classical vocabularies of the Greeks and Romans.

Criticism is perhaps the only process that validates the product of architecture. It is not surprising that the first-century BC building manual *De architectura* (also known as *The Ten Books on Architecture*) by Marcus Vitruvius Pollio, revived after more than fourteen centuries of oblivion, became a basic document of architectural theory with multiples of editions. The first theoretical work in terms of a critical discourse, however, came again under the title of the *Ten Books on Architecture* (originally *De re aedificatoria*; On the Art of Building) by Leon Battista Alberti during the fifteenth century. Alberti, being a practising architect and a man of arts and letters, did not produce solely a didactic book to guide practice, but added substantial depth to the discourse on architecture, which remains unrivalled even today.

Eventually, regular architectural journals appeared. If there were any direct relationship between the quality of architecture and the architectural journal, the first example of this occurred in England. The coverage of architecture in national newspapers and on radio and television, though recently increased in quantity and improved in quality, remains limited and unoriginal. Within the specialist press, however, the subject is generously provided for, at least in comparison to other creative endeavors. The weekly publication now called *Building*, but known for most of its life as *The Builder*, can claim a pedigree going back to the origins of professional journalism in the early Victorian period. After a slightly shaky start in 1842-1843, it hit its stride in 1844 and has been published weekly ever since. We owe the appearance of this journal to its founding editor George Godwin, who published the journal until 1872, for almost forty years, completely by himself.

Critical discourse on architecture cannot be fresh and vivid unless it is communicated through magazines and journals. In recent history, Gio Ponti with *Domus*, Vittorio Gregotti with *Casabella*, Pierre Vago with *L'Architecture d'Aujourdhui* and Kenneth Frampton with *Oppositions* are just a few among those who have left very strong marks on the critical discourse of architecture. In fact, almost every architectural movement starts with a manifesto that is almost immediately associated with a journal. The movement then creates its own constituency, and the critical discourse is propagated. The influential group Archigram began in the early 1960s with a limited edition and home-made magazine voicing the ideas of the group, which the rest of the world of architectural journalism then picked up on.

The Aga Khan's mission in architecture started with a very meticulously developed Award. Immediately after that, the establishment of a journal in order to disseminate the ideas cultivated and the explorations made under the Aga Khan's leadership became a necessity. That is how *Mimar* originated, and it filled an enormous vacuum regarding 'architecture in development' that no institution would address with the depth, breadth and quality given to it by the Aga Khan development network.

Architectural criticism and awards are two processes that validate architecture. But what are the mechanisms that validate criticism or journalism? One mechanism is recognition by bodies from outside the architectural profession. For example, the prestigious American journalism award, the Pulitzer Prize, established a criticism category in 1970. Since then, this criticism prize has been awarded to half a dozen newspaper architectural critics, including Ada Louise Huxtable (1970), Paul Goldberger (1984) and Robert Campbell (1996). Such a prize sets a new target at least for American architectural critics to validate the quality of their contributions.

New developments show that we have reason to be optimistic regarding the recognition of the importance of architectural journalism. For example, the Graham Foundation for Advanced Studies in the Fine Arts recently established the Richard Solomon Award for Architectural Journalism in commemoration of its highly respected director, who passed away in 2005. This award aims to recognise and support excellence in architectural journalism as well as in related professional practices and disciplines.

The Aga Khan Award for Architecture established a most sophisticated and fair process of selection for nominated projects. At the same time, it has recognised the lack of critical thinking on architecture and the scarcity of architectural journalism in the Islamic world. It began addressing this problem as early as 1986, when it organised a seminar in Malta entitled *Criticism in Architecture*. The main mission of the seminar was to bring together notable international editors and critics working in the field of architecture in order to interact with their colleagues from the Muslim world. Since then, plenty of journals addressing architecture have appeared in this part of the world. These not only aim at documenting the accomplishments of our times, but also at cultivating an arena of criticism. In cultures where only declarations of adoration have been accepted, introducing criticism is a hard task to undertake. Nevertheless, critical thinking is developing. This monograph, resulting from the Kuwait seminar *Architectural Criticism and Journalism*, shows how much the field has developed. The Award is proud to give priority to the subject of architectural criticism in the Islamic world, and we sincerely hope that it will be further enhanced by the repercussions of this publication and seminar.

***

The Aga Khan Award for Architecture and the Kuwait Society of Engineers are grateful to the International Committee of Architectural Critics (CICA) for its participation through its most respected and senior members in this venture.

Preface

JASSIM M. QABAZARD, DEPUTY CHAIRMAN, KUWAIT SOCIETY OF ENGINEERS

The Kuwait Society of Engineers (KSE) is honoured to have co-hosted in Kuwait with the Aga Khan Award for Architecture the seminar *Architectural Criticism and Journalism*, from which this publication has emerged.

The seminar, which has brought together a prestigious group of international professionals and experts in the fields of architecture and journalism, could not have happened at a better time as it coincided with the peak of KSE's yearly activities, and may therefore be considered the pinnacle of its events.

The presence of international participants has undoubtedly contributed to enhancing and broadening the exchange of knowledge, thoughts, visions and ideas with their counterparts in Kuwait.

KSE's main theme, entitled "Direction", has aimed at encouraging the development of an awareness of our city. We welcome the opportunity of having this international group of specialists focus their attention on Kuwait.

The city of Kuwait has undergone a radical transformation from its original vernacular architectural state since the late 1940s, when Kuwait became an oil exporting country. The country then began an era of modernisation, and introduced welfare schemes. Unfortunately, one of the drawbacks of Kuwait's recent urban development, growth and prosperity is the disappearance of its traditional urban fabric and past architectural identity. Today, Kuwaitis recognise, with sadness, the injustice we have brought upon our own heritage. Our guests might still be able to catch glimpses of the remains of a few forgotten structures from a once beautiful city of culture, tradition and livelihood that was typical of the architecture of the Gulf region.

I expect that the simple fact of recognising our failure to protect and save our urban heritage will now help provide us with an incentive to restore what is left in a worthy manner. It is here that the contribution of this seminar can be effective for us: it may help set in motion and support our drive towards achieving a 'vision' for the future of Kuwait, and may help us develop guidelines that will identify a suitable 'direction' for implementing that vision.

Introduction.
Predicaments of Architectural Criticism

MOHAMMAD AL-ASAD

An intriguing paradox is the one about the tree falling in a forest and no one is there to hear it fall. Would it make a sound? An acceptable answer is that it would *not* make a sound. The argument supporting this position would be that an act, phenomenon, or object only exists if it has been perceived.

If we extend this line of thinking, which admittedly runs the risk of grossly oversimplifying the rich literature that exists on theories of perception, it may be argued that a work of architecture only exists to those who perceive it. In the case of the vast majority of buildings, the perceivers are those who pass by or use the building. This circle of 'perceivers' is relatively small on the global level, and the vast majority of buildings will eventually disappear completely from the realm of memory after they are torn down or significantly modified. Such a state of affairs, however, changes considerably when a work of architecture is represented through the written word. Even an image of a work of architecture, such as a drawing or photograph, is not very meaningful without an accompanying caption (that is, a text) that explains it. A written account of a building, on the other hand, no matter how brief it may be, crosses the boundaries of space and time. It brings the work of architecture out of its relative anonymity as a local object, and introduces it to a circle of perceivers that is much wider than those who experience the real work of architecture directly through their senses. It also extends the life of the building beyond its physical existence and preserves knowledge of it into the future.

How does such a preamble fit in within the context of architectural criticism? Clearly, not every written representation of a building is a work of criticism. Some writings merely serve the purpose of documentation; some belong to the realm of architectural history; and others are placed under the umbrella of architectural theory. As for architectural criticism, we most often associate it with attempts at explaining and assessing contemporary works of architecture. However, the borders separating criticism from the documentation, history and theory of architecture are hazy. It may also be argued that everyone involved in writing about architecture will eventually end up, to one degree or another, engaging in the act of architectural criticism, that is, explaining and assessing the contemporary built environment around us. I remember when, as a student of architecture, even my most esoterically inclined professors who taught the architecture of geographically and chronologically distant cultures could not resist the occasional temptation to pass judgement (usually negative) on contemporary works of architecture.

The essays in this monograph are primarily about the challenges and opportunities of representing a building through the written word, chiefly in the form of architectural criticism, but also as general writing about architecture. They are also about disseminating that written word to a wide audience, traditionally through the medium of print (newspapers, magazines, journals, monographs, and so on), and, more recently, digitally through the Internet. Of course there is also the audio-visual media of film, radio and television, which may not be the primary venues for reflecting upon architecture, but nonetheless do have a small but important role in disseminating information and opinions on architecture.

This monograph is a unique publication. It brings together contributions by authors who represent considerable geographic and cultural diversity, coming as they do from North and Central America, Europe, Africa, as well as Western, Central, South and East Asia. The publication presents countries where the traditions of writing about architecture are at varying stages of their evolution. In some of these countries, the challenges are still at the level of simply bringing into existence the beginnings of a tradition of printing publications on architecture, often a specialised journal or magazine. Under those circumstances, the emphasis is usually on documenting what is being built; it is difficult to assess what exists before documenting it. In other countries, the challenge lies in securing the survival of existing publications in the face of financial pressures or the indifference of the architectural community. In some cases, editors and publishers also have to deal with the animosity of members of the architectural community, for there will always be architects who feel neglected by the publications around them, and those who perceive the coverage of their work in those publications as negative criticism.

In other countries, architectural publications may exist, and their survival, while not secured, may not face immediate threats. The challenge in such contexts is transforming the emphasis of those publications from being descriptive catalogues to analytical works that evaluate, assess and interpret – in other words, engage in a process of architectural criticism.

In countries with relatively established traditions of architectural criticism, there is often an abundance of publications. While these may not always be able to enjoy the comforts of economic security, a number of them will survive financially at any time. The challenge for these publications is to make the voice of architectural criticism heard, and to make a difference, rather than being relegated to the margins of cultural discourse.

In spite of this wide variety of conditions in which the authors, editors and publishers represented in this monograph have to function, in most of the accounts they provide the prevailing mood is that architectural criticism is in a state of crisis. There is a predominant feeling that 'the word' is not getting out, either because of indifference from what exists of a reading public, or worse (though less often) because of hostility to what is published. In this context, the remarks of author Tom Wolfe in his satirical account of mid-twentieth-century Modern art, *The Painted Word*, are of considerable relevance. Wolfe remarked how an artist such as Jackson Pollock was "pushing his work in the direction" of the writings of critics and theorists such as Clement Greenberg. In this case, the written words of art criticism were not only taken seriously, they were directly influencing (if not dictating) artistic output.[1] Contemporary architectural critics can only react to such an account with envy.

In contrast, the message that strongly comes across in the pages of this monograph is that the options available for architectural critics are often limited to either 'cheerleading' the architectural star of the day, or being relegated to making inaudible remarks from the margins of the world of architecture, assuming a position in that world may be secured.

It seems that contemporary architectural criticism is still in search of a role. This role may be to inform the architect and consequently affect the architectural product (see Pollock and Greenberg above). The role may also be to inform the public, which inevitably will affect the architect and works he or she produces.

Still, there is reason to be optimistic that the written word of criticism can have a serious role in delineating and defining the visual world of the built environment. In this context, the remarks of architectural historian James Ackerman come to mind. Ackerman states that criticism combines response and interpretation.[2] Response is a rather informal and even instinctive reaction to a work of architecture, a reaction that anyone with a developed visual sense is capable of providing. Interpretation, on the other hand, depends on considerable knowledge of the work of architecture and of the technical, sociocultural and economic contexts in which it is produced. Having access to this knowledge allows the creators, perceivers and users of architecture to fully understand its examples and appreciate the levels of complexity that it consciously and subconsciously involves. It is here that the role of the professional critic becomes important. The critic translates, decodes and contextualises the often opaque or mystifying visual languages of architecture through the medium of words. The opportunities for making criticism relevant to architects and to the public at large are abundant. The challenge lies in finding ways of identifying and grasping these opportunities.

[1] See Tom Wolfe, *The Painted Word*, Farrar, Straus & Giroux, New York 1975, pp. 63–64.
[2] See James Ackerman, "Interpretation, Response: Towards a Theory of Art Criticism", in *Distance Points: Essays in Theory and Renaissance Art and Architecture*, MIT Press, Cambridge, Mass. 1991, pp. 37–56.

Contents

Contents (continued)

Contents (continued)

I. INTRODUCING CRITICISM

Architecture and Criticism

FRANÇOIS CHASLIN

Architects are often disappointed by criticism. Many of them say that it does not even exist. But criticism does exist, if only because there are critics – people engaged in the activity. So if critics exist, so does criticism. As Descartes wrote in his *Discourse on Method*, "*cogito, ergo sum*" (I think, therefore I am).

Even so, it is a discipline with vague contours. It concerns professions that are very different in both their aims and methods, as much as in the people who practise them. Some of these professions are complementary, but only up to a certain point. Some of them are involved with the ordinary press (the kind engaged in controversy or information, which is immediate and reacts to events) as much as with long-term historical or theoretical scrutiny, as with university research, for example, which has developed considerably since the 1960s and 1970s. Moreover, all of these activities can take place at the same time and by the same people.

Critics may be journalists or historians, even if the term 'critic' should be reserved for those involved in the analysis of immediate or contemporary production. They may also be teachers or even practising architects. On the one hand, there is fragmentary work concerning architecture or culture – often linked to current events – that addresses the general public as much as the specialist. On the other, there is in-depth work carried out over the long term with goals that are more theoretical or scientific in nature, which is articulated into research work based on a precise methodology. This targets a specialist public, and often requires the exploration of archives and other documentary sources.

Criticism is not strictly identifiable with journalism. It is not limited to merely providing information since it demands that the subject in question be dealt with amongst a broader set of problems. It also requires comparative analysis that is based on a knowledge of both historical and contemporary precedents, thus providing for an approach and for knowledge that are enquiring, even 'philosophical'. Not every journalist is a critic, and there is even a certain form of journalism that refuses critical responsibility and concentrates instead on communication; it is therefore closer to public relations or propaganda than to analysis.

The word 'critic', which comes from the same Greek root that gave us 'crisis', refers to the act of judging or deciding. The word presupposes commentary. Judgement is very much present, with the constant ambition of making discussion more acute, developing it, understanding it, or bringing it into being. At the same time, it supposes a capacity for taking risks. Critics, therefore, have to face a specific type of intellectual responsibility (and sometimes even litigation).

Criticism always means evaluating and placing a work in its historic context and amongst the issues that are contemporary with it, confronting discourse and also the building as it stands. It can be 'critical' in the most ordinary, mordant sense: "sticking the pen into the wound" in the manner of a certain style of journalism – to borrow an expression from the writer Paul Morand.

Criticism is also about the circulation of ideas in the professional world and amongst the public, as much as in the community of architects. This is to say that it has a role to teach and initiate, as well as to interrelate, animate and even structure intellectual debate within the profession. Apart from commenting, critics must explain and bring into contact opinions, viewpoints and cultures.

Criticism often proposes to accompany or channel the evolution of architectural trends, to identify their historical roots, and to elaborate their imaginary or mythical sagas. At a minimum, it needs to make them legible and instrumental, even if that also means making them simplified, prone to amnesia and largely one-voiced.

This is what nineteenth-century critics such as Eugéne Emmanuel Viollet-le-Duc and John Ruskin did. This is also what the theorists of Classicism, Eclecticism and various regionalisms did. More recently, during the twentieth century, this was also true of the historians and critics linked to the Modern Movement, such as Emil Kaufmann, who wanted to draw a line from Ledoux to Le Corbusier; Nikolaus Pevsner, who subjected his judgements to what he thought was a necessary appropriateness to the spirit of the age; and Henry-Russell Hitchcock, who, along with Philip Johnson, popularised the idea of an International Style. It was also the case of engineer and art historian Siegfried Gideon, who was secretary general of the Congrès Internationaux d'Architecture Moderne (CIAM) for thirty years, and who outlined a history of architecture adapted to support the Modern Movement.

In contrast, Lewis Mumford in the United States developed a culture-related view of urban reality that was critical of the theories of Le Corbusier, just as the Danish architect Steen Eiler Rasmussen stood for classic humanist values.

In post-war Italy, Bruno Zevi pleaded for a directly involved experience of space, with violent anti-academic undertones. After defending organic architecture, he became the irascible enemy of Postmodernism.

Then came the contesting of Modernist dogma by the Anglo-Saxon generation of the 1960s: Reyner Banham, who started out in the atmosphere of English Pop and New Brutalism, showed how so-called Functionalism itself proceeded from a formalism of some kind. Other critics of this generation include Colin Rowe, Vincent Scully, Joseph Rykwert and Peter Collins.

After them, during the 1970s, came the theorists – or agitators – marked by the Historicist and Postmodern movements: Manfredo Tafuri, Aldo Rossi, Paolo Portoghesi and Bernard Huet, to mention a few. Some of them were architects, but most were teachers or art historians. It is significant that they were ten to fifteen years younger than the Anglo-Saxons mentioned above. Each generation has its specific task, even if a large part of the production of one generation carries over to the next.

During the mid 1960s, Robert Venturi in the United States invited people to rediscover the virtues of ambiguous compositions. In parallel to the Pop movement, he affirmed the importance of the sign and of contemporary mass culture. At the same time, the Norwegian Christian Norberg-Schulz sought to elaborate a 'logical system' of architecture, one that would integrate the psychology of perception, phenomenology and semantics. Towards the end of his life, he became absorbed by research into the idea of *genius loci*, and was increasingly influenced by Louis Kahn and the philosopher Martin Heidegger.

During the early 1980s, in a reaction against Postmodernism, Kenneth Frampton developed the notion of Critical Regionalism. He called for an enrichment of the universalist values of Modernity by paying closer attention to the specific quality of each place. In this, he wanted to resist the real threat of a general standardisation of models and life styles. He maintained that certain values had survived in isolated schools in regions such as Catalonia and Ticino, and in cities such as Porto and Osaka. Its heroes included Mario Botta, Álvaro Siza and Tadao Ando.

Then came Deconstructivism, with its background of philosophical deconstruction inspired by Jacques Derrida, and its fascination for science via diverse theories of complexity, chaos and catastrophe. This was soon followed by a vogue for non-formal, virtual reality membranes and organic structures. In the domain of urban design came a sweeping new awareness of the raw characteristics of the urban landscape, as with Rem Koolhaas and his generic city, or the more classical Andre Corboz and his palimpsest territory.

Each of these turning points, each of these movements and moments, saw the appearance of a new generation of critics, or changes of views amongst members of the previous generation of critics. Charles Jencks, for instance, who invented the expression "Postmodern" in 1977, some twenty years later published *The Architecture of the Jumping Universe*, which focused entirely on fractals and the butterfly-wing effect.

Critics are carried by their times as much as those times frame them. Their theoretical bases shift. They relate to various spheres: technical and functional thought, aesthetics, history, concern for urban issues, philosophical or political commitment and social critique, and the social sciences. This is evident in the importance to criticism during the 1960s and 1970s of Ferdinand Saussure's linguistics, semiology, Lacanian psychoanalysis, and the entire body of Structuralist thought. Each period valorises one approach or another for global reasons that correspond to the general concerns of society (at least those of intellectual society), and that are often external to architecture proper.

Our age is one of generalised intersubjectivity. In order to exist on the scene in the eyes of public opinion, of critics, and even of colleagues and possible clients, architects (as artists are already in the habit of doing) have to develop their own 'thing', mark their differences and develop an identifiable style.

If the Modern – as has already been the case in the past – is no longer a cause but a style, a manner amongst others of being elegant and of distinguishing one's self, if it is no longer an overall involvement of the individual that commands a broader world view, one articulated to a belief in human or technical progress for example, then what Modern is today becomes fragile, uncertain of its foundations, and more than ever concerned about its own legitimacy.

And if the Postmodern is no longer a combative enterprise and a hard line marking a clear break, if it too has become a simple style, a capacity for juggling with aesthetic fragments, signs and codes borrowed here and there, then even the Postmodern no longer feels itself animated by a historic finality of a higher order. It, therefore, cannot offer itself to our judgement and taste as being anything more than a cultural product of the moment, incapable of arguing further forward or of justifying itself.

Accordingly, the traditional foundations of criticism have been sapped, since there are no longer any causes or systems of general values, and no philosophical authority higher and more noble than simple architectural work on which to base our points of view. We can no longer rationalise our judgements, nor can we refer them to a higher intellectual register.

We are therefore thrown back once and for all into the domain of opinions: opinions that are individual and devoid of cohesion, and that are conscious of being limited to the realm of taste and subjectivity, and even superficiality.

Is architecture like stew then, where an initial quick tasting is enough to tell whether or not it is any good? Certainly not: experience and discussion with architects and non-architects alike show that, for the general public, architecture is an opaque discipline. It usually calls forth either censure or a demand for explanation and commentary. This is no doubt one dimension of contemporary criticism, its pedagogic function as it were.

One sure role of criticism is to share tastes, to dispense the matter of an emotion or the movement of a thought process to those who do not spontaneously feel such things. We might compare it to guiding a blind person so that his or her mental eye opens to the world of plastic, constructive, or cultural forms and articulations that formerly had remained foreign. Initiation and explanation are friendly notions that I prefer to the idea of pedagogy, which supposes that there is a necessary truth to pass on.

This activity of transmitting emotion, of introducing people to a new type of beauty or thought, mode of construction, or set of social problems, entails communicating in very different ways.

The initiation to emotion is a most delicate enterprise. It exposes itself to irony, to excesses in expression or interpretation, and to turgid writing that borders on the ridiculous. The critic has to have a capacity to transcribe, to seek in associations of words the equivalents for uncertain spatial experiences that are fleeting and difficult to talk about, and that may even be imaginary to some extent. What is needed here is not so much an effort of analytical judgement, deciphering and assessment, but rather the translation of what is ineffable, passing from the language of formal and spatial emotions to that of words and sensations that may already be part of the reader's experience, and that we assume he or she will be able to recognise.

The vocation of teaching criticism addresses itself to the general public, in so far as people are interested in the human activity that is architecture. But it also addresses (or at least hopes to address) architects themselves, with their clan-like population, often parochial, little disposed to dialogue, and ill-prepared to understand the work of others.

In these times of rampant individualism, it is helpful to know what sea we are sailing in, to have a map of its archipelagos, and to evaluate the distances that separate us. Even if we have become egotistical individuals, and no longer the valiant little soldiers of progress of bygone days, let us remain communicating individuals all the same.

In this age, the reviews, the media system in general, and even the most demure of architects – even though they may pretend otherwise and whatever their frustrated exasperations may be – are interested mainly in a small cluster of architectural stars, who for one reason or another, and each in his or her own way, have been able to focalise upon themselves a share of current architectural thought.

People at large, including architects, are now more interested in human and artistic types that display ambiguous blends rather than a classic professional profile. And we cannot always tell what derives from genuine skill, and what comes from the narcissistic autobiography of the artist and the fascination that it exerts on the observer.

Today, we are dealing with architects as creators and not anonymous agents in white smocks or technicians of habitat or urbanism who pool their skills in a group effort, a condition to which many people aspired during the 1960s. And so, once again, taste and feeling triumph over reason; excess and brio over realism. The unexpected carries the day before the familiar; innovation floors continuity; and the spectacular outdoes mere professional skill.

Critics may still be able to explain, to comment and debate, to compare and – with a little more difficulty – to cut through and arbitrate; but in no way can they dictate as they did during the days of dogma. They may say that so and so is nothing but an imbecile, a mediocre creator to boot, but they cannot pretend to put the person in question back on the right path since there no longer seems to be one.

The scruples of the 1970s and the spinsters of the revolutionary thought of 1968 still live on, like a grumpy bad conscience that is there to irritate an exuberant young generation with its ever-latent reproaches. The last supporters of urbanity, analysis, history and applied psycho-sociology are a seedy-looking lot; not to mention the militants of more ideological causes: ecologists, participationists, or even town planners and all those ever on the lookout for the conditions of social complexity or possibilities of improving housing.

They have all been swept off the stage, pushed into the wings by the lively, ever-changing production of today, which is self-centred, a little cynical, and essentially emphasises the short term and individualism.

This is the era of advertising and activism, of stress and of marketing communication. It is the era of the image and the logo, of ego exaltation; that of designer and client all in one. Architecture has become a value in its own right and is its own justification. At the same time, it has become an instrument to advertise social groups, cities and regions, political leaders, and big firms. The notion of novelty supplants that of progress, the old desire for revolution is replaced by constant change that implies inflow and outflow and does not postulate that there is a horizon bounding our actions, a higher goal, or that we should aspire to anything other than whichever trend is leading us as it pleases.

No wonder criticism often descends to publicity and mere praise. In our media-dominated age, even architectural production is convinced that it has to produce as many theories as there are individuals. It nourishes a pseudo-criticism that is mercenary by nature. Real criticism, the kind that looks for meaning, is made all the more difficult. It has to sift through a period that is a slave to the star system, to affected artists' postures, to eclecticism with no real philosophical foundation, to the coexistence of individualities rather than pluralism, and to the weakening of general opinions and positive ideologies.

There is also the universal problem of communication as a system, with its press attachés, general control of information, intimidation, flattery, invitations and small gifts. And I need not insist on the salaried relationships that make certain critics the employees of the architects they talk about, or of the various institutions that pay them to take part in discussions and seminars, or to write texts, reports and communiqués. It may not be straightforward bribery, but the concordance of interests is clear.

Criticism and Virtue

JOSEPH RYKWERT

If our professional father Marcus Vitruvius Pollio (active 46–30 BC) is to be believed, some of the earliest human speech was architectural criticism. The accidental discovery of a forest fire and the comfort it gave them led men to come together in societies, in which they communicated first with gesture and inarticulate noises. In articulating them, they had created language.

The discovery of fire, he says in his treatise *De architectura*:

> Led to the coming together of men [...] who, finding themselves naturally gifted above other animals, and not obliged to walk with faces to the ground, but upright – so that they were able to look on the splendour of the starry sky and were able to deal easily with whatever they wanted by using hands and fingers –, began to build shelters as soon as they came together.[1]

These shelters, so Vitruvius thought, were made of boughs or dug in caves or yet of mud and twigs, imitating swallows' nests. Observing the shelters others made, he goes on:

> And adding new details of their own invention, with time they constructed ever better huts. And being of an imitative and teachable nature they pointed out the results of their building daily to each other, boasting of the novelties they invented. As their natural gifts were sharpened by emulation, their buildings improved daily.[2]

This mythical account of the origin of building incorporates criticism into its invention. How could the first buildings have improved without mutual criticism, he seems to imply. Criticism is therefore a primal element of speech; and in building, it is an essential part of the building process.

Of course, the kind of architectural criticism that we practise nowadays is only indirectly related to such mythic origins. It is carried by forms of printing (as with books and newspapers) and by various electronic media. Many newspapers employ regular architectural critics, as do some radio and television programmes.

In this proliferation, I recall our beginnings to affirm the continuity of the process: the only way to escape architectural criticism is to avoid building. Like those fire-watchers in Vitruvius' account, everyone has an opinion about buildings, especially new ones. And not all buildings are worthy of critical attention, nor should critics be attended to. I would like to suggest that there are two elements that validate criticism, whether we agree with it or not.

The first is a theoretical structure behind or within which it will act as a backbone to individual judgements. Do not believe a critic who tells you he can dispense with any theory: that only means he has a bad one, which he may well be unwilling to expose to daylight.

Any theory must be rooted in history: what has already been built is a treasure we need to consult and revalue constantly. Any worthwhile theory will have to serve us as a guide among the buildings of the past, illuminate our preferences, but also show us how to value past achievements against each other, and how to distinguish dross (of which there has always been plenty) from what is of value. That is the essence of our activity, after all: discrimination. The very title of critic we have assumed looks back to the act of winnowing, of separating the grain from the worthless chaff that the wind will blow away.

There can be no theory of the future: we can only theorise by extrapolating from past experience – which is why futurology, a once popular science that ran on techno-optimism until energy crises intervened, has now fallen into disfavour. And we can only foretell by extrapolation: which works well enough in calculating short-term financial risks, for instance, but is not much use in counselling long-term strategic choice. Strategy, after all, is not about what will inevitably happen, but about how to achieve a desired outcome.

Desire, even love, are therefore the key to criticism. We look back at the past – even the most recent past – and we examine, interpret and recommend the things we love to our audience. There is no history without love – and hate. History is the second element that drives our activity. We form our theories in the light of what we have learned from the past, and we judge the past by the light of our theories, which will speak to us about the relation between the building and its inhabitants, the building and its environment, and the internal structure of the building – both physical and formal.

I have not said anything about aesthetics. They seem to be only marginally interesting to architectural criticism, since – in so far as they are an independent discipline – they can only tell us something about the spectator's sensory reaction to a building, while all the other factors I have mentioned seem to me very much more important both to the architect and to his client.

---

[1] Adapted from *Vitruvius: The Ten Books on Architecture*, translated by Morris Hicky Morgan, Dover Publications, New York 1960, II 1, ii.

[2] Adapted from *Vitruvius: The Ten Books on Architecture* cit., II 1, iii.

Architectural Criticism: History, Context and Roles

DENNIS SHARP

The criticism of architecture is concerned with, and to a large extent dependent upon, knowledge. A good critic will have an understanding of history and theory. However, it is a discipline in itself that relies upon skills, information and knowledge deriving from history, theories, aesthetics, as well as social values and sources. It is a distinct area of production, although often aggravated by external factors, such as editors' and publishers' deadlines.

An architectural critic without a real understanding of architectural and environmental history is like a lion without a tail. Historical and theoretical knowledge cannot be flicked away. For the well-known contemporary editor and critic Ernesto Rogers, to understand history was "essential for the formation of the architect", and of course those who write about architecture – whom we refer to as 'critics' – need to have the same understanding. The critic's role is also personal, interpretative and quite often subjective. Criticism has to be honest.

ARCHITECTURAL CRITICISM

Architectural criticism has a history. It may be a fairly recent professional activity, but its roots lie deep in the past. It is literally being knowledgeable about and critical of a work, an artefact, or an idea, for good or bad. Criticism of course should be constructive, but, equally, it could be the opposite and destroy the reputation of a building, a project, an idea, or even a person.

The historical origins of modern architectural criticism, relating to aesthetic judgement, issues and values, came to the surface during the mid nineteenth century. It was German art historians at the turn of the twentieth century, such as Jacob Burckhardt, Heinrich Wölfflin, Wilhelm Worringer and August Schmarsow, who helped establish the bases of modern architectural criticism. In the nineteenth century, John Ruskin was a frequent commentator and critic of architecture, as well as of architectural styles and values. Compare his views on Venice and the Gothic. He was an ethical critic rooted in nineteenth-century fundamentalist Christian values. Ruskin was speaking to an audience of students at the Architectural Association (AA) in London in 1857 when he said about criticism: "Keep yourselves quiet, peaceful, with your eyes open [...] The anxiety whether Mr So and So will like your work is not a wrong feeling but impertinent and wholly incompatible with the full exercise of your imagination."[1] In Ruskin's view, "Beauty" and "Truth" were inseparable as architecture has a high moral value.

The autonomy of modern architectural criticism derives from those who promoted the new, rational Modern architecture. Their views were often specific, ideological and thought to be socially and ethically sustained. Walter Gropius wrote in 1935 that a "modern building should derive its architectural significance from the vigor and consequence of its own organic proportions. It must be true to itself, logically transparent, and virginal of lies and trivialities."[2] This was a critique of contemporary production, but with the demise of Modernism, followed by the Postmodernist phase in the 1970s, it proved untenable.

There is, however, a need to distinguish between the architect, architectural historian, theorist, teacher, journalist, writer-author, and the architectural commentator or documentarian as critic.

A huge diversity of backgrounds of architectural critics is to be found in the twentieth century. Architectural circles that range from practising architects, editors, to philosophers have included Siegfried Gideon, Herbert Read, Lewis Mumford, J. M. Richards, Gillo Dorfles, Bruno Zevi, William Jordy, Paul Zucker, Pierre Vago, Reyner Banham, Charles Jencks, Julius Posener and Joseph Rykwert, to name a few.

ROLE, CONTEXT AND PURPOSE OF ARCHITECTURAL CRITICISM

The positive role of criticism is basically to inform, educate, clarify, compare and define 'quality' based on the knowledge of a project from the initial conceptual design phase to completion and into active use, as well as to examine the project's social use and 'context'.

The words 'context' and 'contextualism' crept into architectural vocabulary during the late 1960s as part of the first substantial critique of the post-war phase of Modern architecture. It began in Italy during the mid 1950s when Ernesto Rogers in *Casabella* bemoaned the fact that architects treated their buildings as "unique abstractions indifferent to location and context". He claimed that in Modern architecture there was no dialogue with a building's surroundings, that is, what he called a pre-existent ambient.

British historians Adrian Forty[3] and John Onions have observed that, in architecture, the first consciously developed 'linguistic criticism' appeared with the publication in 1575 of Sebastiano Serlio's *Treatise on Architecture*. More recently, much study has gone into architectural history on the 'gendering' of architecture (principally the Orders) as well as the articulation of form, surface and space. Gender theory looks at the masculine ideas of the eighteenth-century French architect Jacques-François Blondel and the American architect Louis Sullivan (d. 1924), but soon loses itself in the Modernist period. Forty suggests that gender metaphors ran counter to Modernist tenets. This was so – even to critics out of sympathy with Modernism.

The context of architectural criticism is wide. When the Comité International des Critiques d'Architecture (CICA) was founded in 1979, there was little interest in the subject. At that time, two major areas of concern emerged. The first was the lack of published architectural features and criticism in national papers and journals, particularly in comparison with the coverage afforded to other arts, including film, literature, theatre, dance, sculpture and painting. The other area was concerned with the contribution architectural critics could make to architectural practice, as well as with the development of project designs, particularly through an involvement in offering advice for the development of international competition entries, as well as the renovation and preservation of historic buildings, and the design of public ones.

The critical apparatus of Modernism derives from the languages of form developed by the great German philosophers Immanuel Kant (d. 1804) and Georg Wilhelm Friedrich Hegel (d. 1831), and reiterated and expanded by Heinrich Wölfflin (d. 1945) and Worringer, the successors of the art historian Johann Joachim Winckelmann (d. 1768). In England, another tradition of encapsulated history and architectural and social comment emerged, often laced with a deeply religiously felt ethical zeal pursued by Ruskin in his critical attack not only on Classicism in general, but also on the 1851 Great Exhibition's prefabricated Crystal Palace in London.

The nineteenth-century historian James Fergusson was an amateur and more objective critic of historical trends, and had an interest in early international vernacular architecture (before the term was widely used). He claimed that Modern buildings were "very unsatisfactory".

The famous German architect and writer Hermann Muthesius (d. 1927) was himself a widely published critic. He commented on trends (see *The English House*) and positions in architecture at the turn of the twentieth century. He later began exploring the concepts of Modernity in a wide European context from his Berlin base, and was one of the founding fathers of the Deutscher Werkbund, the association devoted to the development of German handiwork and industrial work.

These 'critics' were, in many cases, also art and social historians.

TYPES OF CRITICISM AND CRITICS
Critical methodologies are based on criteria such as aesthetics, construction, cultural values, form, shape and materials. Some years ago, I introduced a number of critical categories in the *Architectural Journalism and Criticism Workshop* to the Architectural Association. These categories related to an ungraded list of criteria. They were neither simply a series of categories nor a foolproof checklist. Rather they were an attempt to create a working tool whereby students' ideas, thoughts and words could be focused on the main areas that criticism might be expected to cover.

The list was divided into dualities: environmental/economic, functional/constructional, political/cultural, and of course visual/aesthetic categories. Some of these areas overlapped while others were added later in an effort to create a more fluid critical process. This helped greatly in providing clarification for the aims and content of the critical writing undertaken by the students. It formed a basis for sharpening arguments and for opening up widely differing areas of knowledge. In its simplest form, the categories could become paragraph headings. We also used them in discussions, and in the course publications produced by the students themselves. The students were rewarded with the publication of articles on major buildings, including the 1960s Economist Building, London, by Peter and Alison Smithson, and another work of their own choice. The results were published in *Building* magazine, where one of the students became an architecture editor.

The young amateur architecture critics soon recognised that the so-called critical and investigative structure of much journalism is related to the 'aesthetic' touchstone that could be defined as the basic ingredient of criticism itself. They no longer needed me to labour the point. They had recognised that it is from the realm of aesthetic appearances that the most productive criticism emanates. It is not without its dangers. Often, aesthetic values – arguments say of the 'appearance' of a project – may be seen as a safe harbour that might exclude use or social purposes. It can become a shelter for the critic's own prejudices and the pursuance of idiosyncratic opinions: witness the diatribes in which many writers engage in those flashy jargon-filled, obtuse and often over-designed student or institutional journals.

THE ROLE OF ARCHITECTURE CRITICS AND THE MEDIA
The purpose of architectural criticism is to bring to a wider reading public – through newspapers, journals, broadcasts and books – informed, independent, objective and critical commentaries on buildings and environment issues. The main vehicles for the dissemination of this information are:

- newspapers
  In most Western papers, the critic of architecture works within the framework of the papers' cultural pages, although there are some exceptions such as *The Financial Times*, where the architectural correspondent is still part of the news team. In newspapers and magazines, architecture is often related to lifestyles or home and property sections news.

  Roles vary considerably and include reporting on and about buildings: new or renovated, experimental and innovatory; interviewing architectural personalities; covering events such as architectural exhibitions; reviewing books and media coverage; and so on.

- architectural journals
  Magazines range from the specialist technical weekly, monthly and quarterly publications of in-

dependent commercial publishers, to those official journals of institutions and building industry sources. In fact, the *RIBA Journal* of the Royal Institute of British Architects and the *Architectural Record* of the American Institute of Architects (AIA) are two of the largest circulation architectural journals in the world that go to members and lay subscribers.

Additionally, there are the academic journals, almost all with international readerships, often serving academic communities. They publish criticism alongside history and theory, an approach pioneered by magazines such as the *AA Quarterly* (1968–1982), which was eventually succeeded by *AA Files*, *ARQ*, *Perspecta*, and so on.

The large circulation popular magazines have different angles from those of the technical, commercial and institutional type. They often produce features and news items on architecture, but in their architectural features employ the leading critics of the day. These magazines include *Architectural Digest*, *Casa Vogue*, *Wallpaper*, *Blueprint* and *Domus*.

Today, things are changing rapidly. In addition to all these printed outlets, a revolution in media outlets has taken place addressing criticism to an enormous public via the Internet. Huge opportunities arise for architectural critics and writers in order to market Internet sites, videos, films, CDs and DVDs devoted to architecture. CICA, which over the last twenty years has had an enormous influence on the development of architectural criticism, now enjoys the freedom offered by the Internet with its web site (www.cicarchitecture.org), which offers features and articles on new buildings, and on architectural history and theory by its members.

The website referenced in this essay was accessed in May 2006.

[1] John Ruskin, "Influence of Imagination in Architecture", in *The Two Paths*, Smith, Elder and Co., London 1859, p. 180.
[2] Cited in Gillian Naylor, *The Bauhaus Reassessed*, New York 1985, p. 132.

[3] Adrian Forty, *Words and Buildings: A Vocabulary of Modern Architecture*, Thames & Hudson, London 2004.

II. REFLECTIONS ON CRITICISM

Architectural Criticism and Civic Society

OMAR AKBAR

Any attempt at formulating the relationship between architecture and architectural criticism requires some introduction. A number of differing perspectives and material attitudes concerning such things as the notion of space, technology, or cognition theory may be adopted with some measure of justification. My intention here, however, is to illuminate the aspect of civic and social significance, and the debate about strengthening elementary values and attitudes. The status enjoyed by such virtues – like the capacity to criticise – or basic social convictions – like the individual's right to self-determination – is of particular importance, especially today. It would therefore appear legitimate to examine the relationship between architecture and architectural criticism for signs of any overriding matters of substance. After all, a political public that has an 'institutionalised capacity to criticise' is one of the core elements of the democratic idea, and any civic culture depends on making actual use of this valuable asset. Art and design – and hence architecture itself – are ultimately aimed at facilitating an aesthetic experience that has the power to change our lives. One therefore may be permitted to assume that a critical dialogue with architecture is an inherent feature of our culture, and that we are dealing with an architectural criticism that really does function freely and independently as a cultural corrective to building activities.

Appropriate, pretentious, or just outdated? The initial findings of our inquiry are straightforward. The role proposed here is not performed by architectural criticism at all. A reflective dialogue with the built environment, with this aim in mind, occurs only in exceptional cases.

It would be easy to say that even the greatest democracies experience difficulties in bringing forth a 'critical public'. And the discussion as to whether this unfortunate circumstance may be remedied would fill whole libraries. We are told there is no way of changing such a state of affairs, and one should therefore set oneself modest goals. Two things may be said about this. First of all, a clear 'Nevertheless' must be stated firmly. The circumstances outlined above go right to the core of every civic culture, and they are closely bound up with our identity and with values such as self-fulfilment and freedom. Secondly, architectural criticism cannot in fact perform this role, because of circumstances that are of its own making and its own fault, but that are also remediable.

Architecture may rightly be seen as a manifestation of our social striving and a reflection of our social reality. Although it plays these important roles, it tends to be treated with a certain superficiality. In other contexts, it even becomes a preferred object of destruction – whether through property speculation, refurbishment through demolition, social frustration, or war. It appears that disdain must also be included among the achievements of our civilisation.

To whom is architectural criticism addressed, and who does it reach? Architectural criticism is a discourse among professionals, recruited mainly from the ranks of its own discipline and a few related professions. Beyond assigning such labels as 'beautiful', 'ugly', 'cosy', and so on – and one may say this without meaning to be arrogant or being guilty of any disrespect –, a large section of the public has little interest in architectural and town planning matters. To this must be added the fact that knowledge of architectural issues is very limited, and that architecture leads a Cinderella existence in general educational curricula. This is an irritating state of affairs when one considers that we are constantly surrounded by architecture and exposed daily to its intense influence.

Another important factor in the interplay between architecture and criticism concerns the architecture that critics choose to discuss. It is striking that everyday architecture – architecture that determines our daily experience – is barely acknowledged. It is understandable that architectural criticism must attract readers, viewers and listeners. What is needed are occasions and topics that arouse curiosity, stir emotions, give rise to astonishment, or provoke reactions. Given that the possibilities of attracting attention are limited, everyday architecture inevitably will be discounted from the start. Architecture generally becomes interesting only when prominent buildings are involved, when so-called 'star architects' make their appearance, or when – banal as it may be – there are scandals or accidents to report. As a result, the building sometimes fades into the background. The architecture that affects us the most gets the least attention.

Reports and commentaries are often incomplete. Important aspects of the social and economic context in which architecture comes into being remain hidden. The relationships between politics, architectural creation, power and intrigue, for example, are seldom presented as an issue. When the results of competitions for public buildings are announced, the media is given the opportunity to scrutinise the designs submitted and to criticise them. But as soon as the project enters the preparatory phase of implementation, things get murky. The process extending from the design competition invitation to the completion of the end product cannot be critically observed and followed by the public. Modifications made at a later stage cannot be explained. Only in the final phase can criticism engage in a dialogue with architecture again, albeit only with the end product. The modifications, which are often not determined by the architect, usually disappear from the critic's field of vision. The balance between aspiration, transparency and responsibility is disturbed.

Architectural criticism passes over – in complete silence – so many types of architecture that are significant for our everyday lives. Largely without interest for both critics and architects, for example, are works of architecture without architects. This applies especially to the slum architecture of megacities, which is built by its users. Although these works have highly specific structural, spatial and aesthetic qualities, and although many millions of people live in them, they are ignored.

But architecture, too, largely follows similar global developments and seldom shows much respect for local conditions. It is a product of the zeitgeist and of current trends. If we leave aside the so-called star architects with their individual architectural language, which can lead to a kind of branding, what we see in the world is a mass-produced architecture: monotonous, anonymous, unimaginative and irresponsible – and above all not subject to criticism.

It is in the city, where great cultural values have been created, that criticism of architecture, which has a highly 'civilisatory' value, is too selective. We are in danger of abandoning our basic attitude to civilisation in this very sensitive area. In doing so, we undermine such basic values as criticism and democracy, which have determined the face of the city and civic society since ancient times. The Enlightenment taught us not to accept anything uncritically. Freedom of speech and opinion are among the basic prerequisites for advances in cognition and reason. Criticism and democratic structures have always been among the engines of development. It is these forces that first made open, pluralist thinking possible, as well as thinking in terms of visions and utopias. Architectural criticism can only succeed if it is seen as a reflective dialogue with the built environment, as a form of criticism that does not operate selectively in response to economic constraints, ideologies, or superficial trends. The actors involved always confront the public with a motionless and permanent product. It cannot be deleted, shaken off, or rearranged. Architects, critics and clients have to realise their responsibility for the civic values they each represent by making themselves and the public more sensitive to fundamental values and attitudes.

Architectural Criticism: Thinking Thinner, Deeper and Wider

AYDAN BALAMIR

INTRODUCTION

There is an old saying connecting the three states of matter with the professions of engineering, architecture and planning. Accordingly, engineering represents the solid state, architecture the liquid state, and planning the gaseous state. If I may extend the metaphor to the subject of this publication, then the culture of criticism marks the gaseous state of our liquid profession. There must be great potential in that gas, however, regardless of its limited power to transform the world. The seminar out of which this publication has emerged aimed at discussing the role of criticism in influencing the negligible percentage of buildings designed by architects in a world of growing philistinism on the one hand, and human miseries – poverty, war and natural disasters – on the other. What architectural criticism looks after is refinement and depth in the architectural product, against all the visual pollution around us. It also has a much wider scope of understanding disparities or gaps between excesses and shortages. Criticism can be expected to set up bridges, in the sense of creating means of communication and understanding between seemingly unbridgeable spans and entities, or means of reconciling their differences.

This paper focuses on three gaps that concern architectural criticism, referring roughly to three types of journalism: first, the gap between celebrity – or 'star' – architecture and ordinary practice; second, the gap between the Modernist ethic and market-based production; and third, the gap between academic interests and the real world of practice. The publications that may be clustered around these issues include monographs and architectural journals that disseminate architectural culture; vanity and marketing publications (including interior decoration and real estate magazines) that promote commodities and services in the field; and finally, publications for professional education/instruction and general readership (including technical books and journals, design manuals, and architectural films, videos, and so on).

CELEBRATED ARCHITECTURE AND ORDINARY PRACTICE

The disparity between celebrated architecture and ordinary practice – or stars and satellites – is becoming more visible. One sets the norms of architectural thinking and production; the other reproduces itself within the constraints of regular practice, either carrying on with conventional forms of practice, or imitating the norm-setters at varying levels of competence.[1] As the celebrity mechanism demands constant novelty at all costs, design ideas are rapidly consumed. Quality publications in cultural capitals of the world take the lead in promoting new concepts and techniques, while their lower rate versions find their ways into the peripheries. There is nothing unusual or deeply disturbing about such disparity; coexistence of so-called 'star architecture' and everyday architecture postulates a division that is fundamental to the nature of artistic production. In his cult book *The Shape of Time*, George Kubler considers such division as typical behaviour, referring to how a generally beautiful or distasteful object merely calls for repetition or avoidance. The distinction is put as follows:

> Prime objects and replications denote principal inventions, and the entire system of replicas, reproductions, copies, reductions, transfers and derivations, floating in the wake of an important work of art. The replica-mass resembles certain habits of popular speech, as when a phrase spoken upon the stage or in a film, and repeated in millions of utterances, becomes part of the language of a generation and finally a dated cliché.[2]

Prime objects resemble the prime numbers of mathematics, according to Kubler, while all others bear a mutant gene or fraction by which we can follow the progeny of the prime object. It is among the tasks of architectural history and criticism to identify the progeny of works, unfolding their distinctions and values, in order to identify the field's stars and satellites. The value of foreground works is undisputable for the flourishing of architectural culture. However, the struggle for visibility in today's image-based culture is often criticised for its detachment from social and contextual considerations, for displaying "an air of self satisfaction and omnipotence", as Juhani Palasmaa argues: "Buildings attempt to conquer the foreground instead of creating a supportive background for human activities and perceptions".[3] The accompanying publicity about the sophistication and profundity of the works displayed is convincing so long as deeper questions of humanity are ignored.

The star architecture promoted in seductive monographs and journals creates new objects of desire among young architects and students. Leafing through glossy books and magazines, they are fascinated with images, especially with the innovative blobs and mollusc-like forms of the current avant-garde. Based on pictorial acquaintance alone, the fascination leads to crude imitation, devoid of the conceptual breadth and technical refinement that the original might possess. The abundance of images in architectural publications is only natural; decent photography and drawings are necessary supplements for presenting architectural works. It is the commercial computer-generated renderings that diminish the value of images, providing facile results. In Turkey, this trend has given rise to a new practice of design in the hands of glib professionals with knowledge of computer rendering programs such as 3d studio max™. Nevertheless, the connection of legible line drawings with photographs is still central in established journals, where serious criticism takes place alongside commentaries and post-occupancy evaluations.[4] Without concession from their discriminating eyes, leading books and journals deal not only with flashy foreground buildings, but also with notable examples from among works that stay humbly in the background.

The promotion devices and rituals of architecture are carried also to the digital world today. The medium of architectural criticism is shifting hands. The emergence of weblogs, together with their independent blogging awards, points to a new direction in the dissemination of creative ideas and criticism, stressing publicness, urban architecture and a holistic view of design fields.[5] Architectural blogs have gained increasing popularity, especially among younger generations, with their role in breaking the formalities of printed matter and allowing wide accessibility and portability. "In our digital age, presence and portability are everything", says the editor of the weblog *Tropolism*; it is claimed that formats of printed publications, such as monumentally-sized monographs or encased multi-volumes, do not provide a powerful companion for the reader.[6] As the prospect of such new forms of publication is towards a more interactive 'open architecture' format, it is conceivable in the near future to have them challenging the establishment more radically.

MODERNIST DESIGN ETHIC AND MARKET-BASED PRODUCTION
The second gap in architectural criticism is between the Modernist ethic and market-based production. The distinction between prime objects and reproductions presents a core difference in architectural culture. The world of reproductions consists of considerable variations in design approaches and quality. Shaped by market demands, circumstances of practice and the capacities of professionals, architectural mainstreams may have local variations, or may be in the wake of their counterparts fashioned in the world centres. California-type suburban houses are very well marketed in Turkey, for instance, and the contempt for them that the country's professional elite expresses has not limited their popularity. The predominantly Modernist ethic of well-trained architects is not compatible with cliental demands, nor with the market rules that shape many investments. However, the gap between the design ethics of professionals and popular taste cultures may not be as sharp as in the heyday of architectural Modernism, as the state of current architecture indicates.

Mainstream architecture in Turkey, following a period of uninspiring and generic Modernism, nowadays draws a general profile of ersatz architecture – various sorts of figured bodywork in glass-metal-granite combinations on the one hand, and historicist or regionalist pastiche on the other. Design with commercial facade systems or the ready-made curtain wall has become the new vernacular of Modern architecture, resulting in unimaginative looks and low-end performances. Promoted as 'intelligent' building, the relatively higher-end versions in fact display very limited intelligence or environmental ethics. The pastiche tradition with Classical trappings is much older in architectural culture; the new art of 'antiquifying', so to speak, portrays a return of the nineteenth-century climate worldwide. With the decline of the Modernist ethic and the rise of various specialised construction sectors in architecture, the idea that building exteriors may be decorated to the taste of the client recently found acceptance in Turkey. Only about two decades ago, historical styling of new buildings was almost unthought-of, and if anyone ever thought of it, no 'cosmetic' industry existed for its execution, nor did the accompanying publications for its promotion.

Architecture based on metallic bodywork and plastic or stucco surgery shares more or less the same carcass, the conventional reinforced concrete frame and brick infill behind all the intended glamour. Upon this generic frame, professional territories are drawn. As the title 'interior architect' became more familiar to the public, its counterpart 'exterior architect' has been coined as a new term in the Turkish language. The designer architect is replaced by the professional assembly team of the architectural firm at best. Otherwise, the lay contractor manages the design with ready-made facade systems or decorative paraphernalia. The demand for quality architecture remains meagre in Turkey, despite the existence of vast construction and decoration sectors capable of managing both the import and export of products and services. The equally vast sector of architectural journalism has several cultured magazines with critical contents, against many cut-and-paste journals living on sector advertisement. A number of vanity journals promote 'good living' to the upper classes, their interest being more on decoration and chic places. As for marketing and real estate publications, the majority of material displayed in them constitutes what today needs to be kept in check.

ACADEMIC INTEREST AND THE WORLD OF PRACTICE

The gap between academic interests or the intellectual world on the one hand, and the real world of practice on the other has been stressed by many who have thought about the nature of design and its education.[7] Referring to the institutionalised separation of research from practice, Donald Schön's diagnosis was a "dilemma of rigor or relevance", where academic respectability and social or professional relevance stand in sharp contrast:

> In the geography of professional practice, there is a very dry, high ground where you can use the theories on which you got your Ph.D. Down below is a swamp where the real problems live. The difficulty is to decide whether to stay in the high ground, where you can be rigorous but deal with problems of lesser importance, or go down into the swamp to work on problems you really care about but in a way you see as hopelessly unrigorous.[8]

The dilemma was implied in Herbert Simon's view of academic subject matter as "intellectually tough, analytic, and formalisable", whereas much of what was known about design in the past was "intellectually soft, intuitive, informal and cookbooky".[9] The so-called cookbooks of architecture were varied; apart from classical manuals, there were popular composition books, for instance, which were belittled by the Modern movement for being at the disposal of the mediocre mind. However, these books contained a truly relevant and instrumental body of knowledge to aid the lesser architect and prevent banalism in average architectural production. They contained, in the terminology of the late philosopher of science Thomas Kuhn, "concrete problem solutions" by which the members of the professional community learned their tasks. In his critical survey of those composition books, Colin Rowe drew attention to their pedagogic value:

> Sharing a common critical vocabulary, and apparently enjoying a common visual experience, their writers were preoccupied with the survival of certain standards of urbanity and order, the quality of which they recognized as correct composition.[10]

The idea of composition is rather narrow for today's architectural thinking, yet the need for design codes to raise the standards of average practice persists. Bruno Zevi, despite being so critical about the tyranny of frozen codes in Neoclassical architecture, argued for the necessity of a codified language, if it is to be spoken fluently and correctly by the average members of the profession. He believed that its absence is leading to "confusion and anxiety", especially among students of architecture, who are "bewildered by the fact that nobody teaches them an idiom they can speak".[11] With some exaggeration, the argument points to a shortcoming: although the corpus of visual ideas introduced to the student today has grown enormously, the moral-practical knowledge necessary to materialise them seems to have shown no proportionate development. With visual culture alone, the novice can hardly acquire in-depth knowledge to reach expected professional standards of architectural production. The emerging illiteracies breed incompetent maniera in the practice, alongside shallow feats and narrow expediencies. In academia, outwardly the only seat of refinement, depth and breadth of knowledge, scholarly research, and the tendency towards intellectual dilettantism and esotericism hamper the production of substantial knowledge that might permeate the world of practice.

There is relatively little know-how in architectural publications. Technical journals that delve into the anatomy of building design, rather than merely deal with its conceptual stages, are helpful in this respect. Electronic libraries based upon the use of CD-ROMs or online communication networks appear as another promising instrument in raising standards. The field of architectural video production is not as developed as in the music or film industry, even though it has a potential for providing the practising architect with a valuable compendium of architectural culture and technical know-how.

QUESTIONS FOR RESPONSIBLE CRITICISM
Today's avant-garde is rather detached from social concerns, especially when compared to the early Modernist avant-garde, which was based on radical criticism and utopianism. Therefore, almost unspoken of nowadays in the field of criticism is the architecture for the poor or for the victims of war and disaster, and the role of criticism in transforming the world of poverty, overt and concealed.

According to the United Nations, almost one billion people live in slums today. If nothing is done, this number will probably reach two billion by 2020.[12]

Questions of direct relevance to the design professions and their critics are increasingly along the following lines: How might globalisation work for the benefit of humanity, with the design and planning professions contributing towards a culturally, economically and environmentally sustainable future for the urban poor? How can the scope of criticism be expanded as an interdisciplinary endeavour, addressing broad questions of social and ecological relevance? Can critical effort regain authenticity and mercy for humanity? We are immersed in a thrilling millennium that leaves us asking a critical question: "What is the future of our profession?" Alberto Campo Baeza says, "I believe that the future will be grounded in an architecture that is deep rather than shallow, wise rather than witty, logical rather than ingenious – one based on structures capable of constituting architectural space. An architecture that masters gravity and light, that endures and is capable of remaining in the memory of mankind."[13]

All the websites referenced in this essay were accessed in May 2006.

[1] The "star system" in current architecture is widely discussed in the journal *Arredamento Mimarlık*, 187, January 2006, pp. 32–47, especially in the articles (in Turkish) by Ugur Tanyeli and Abdi Güzer.

[2] George Kubler, *The Shape of Time: Remarks on the History of Things*, Yale University Press, New Haven and London 1962, p. 39.

[3] Juhani Palasmaa, excerpts from "Hapacity and Time - Discussion of Haptic, Sensuous Architecture", in *The Architectural Review*, 217: 1297, March 2005, p. 81 (original text was published in *The Architectural Review*, 207: 1239, May 2000).

[4] The list of such publications having worldwide impact includes foremost, established magazines such as *The Architectural Review*, *Architectural Record*, *Architects' Journal*, *L'Architecture d'Aujourd'hui*, *Domus* and *El Croquis*, to name a few. In Turkey, leading magazines include *Yapi* and *Arredamento Mimarlık*.

[5] Such online publications include *Tropolism*, *Infosthetics*, *Interactivearchitecture*, *lifewithoutbuildings*, *Bldgblog*, *Anarchitecture*, *Polis* and *Architechnophilia*.

[6] The quotation is taken from Chad Smith's online review of *Enric Miralles Works and Projects 1975 -1995*, Benedetta Tagliabue Miralles (ed.), in *Tropolism*. See www.tropolism.com/2005/11/tropolism_books_enric_miralles.php. The New York blog *Tropolism* www.tropolism.com) was nominated by its readers for the World's Best Urban Architecture Blog in 2005.

[7] The points covered in this section were previously discussed in: Aydan Balamir, "Theory and Practice in Tandem: Conditions of a Meritocratic System in Architectural Education, Re-Integrating Theory and Design in Architectural Education", in *Proceedings of 19th EEAE International Conference, Transactions on Architectural Education*, Nur Çağlar (ed.), no. 11, 2001, pp. 43–69.

[8] Donald A. Schön, "The Architectural Studio as an Exemplar of Education for Reflection in Action", in *JAE*, 38, 1, autumn 1984, pp. 2–9.

[9] Herbert A. Simon, *The Sciences of the Artificial*, MIT Press, Cambridge, Mass. 1969, pp. 56–57.

[10] Colin Rowe, "Character and Composition; or Some Vicissitudes of Architectural Vocabulary in the Nineteenth Century", in *The Mathematics of the Ideal Villa and Other Essays*, MIT Press, Cambridge, Mass. 1983, pp. 59–88.

[11] Bruno Zevi, *The Modern Language of Architecture*, University of Washington Press, Seattle 1978, p. 5.

[12] From the website of The Global Studio, held in 2005 in Istanbul as part of the UIA 2005 - Istanbul World Architecture Congress. See www.theglobalstudio.com/00_Home/00_Home.htm. The Global Studio programme was based on the principles laid out in "The United Nations Millennium Project's Task Force to Improve the Lives of Slum Dwellers".
See www.unmillenniumproject.org.

[13] Alberto Campo Baeza, excerpt in *10x10_2: 100 Architects 10 Critics*, Phaidon Press, Oxford 2005, pp. 409–410.

The Conundrums of Architectural Criticism

TREVOR BODDY

Everyone likes the idea of architectural criticism. Far fewer like the actual practice of architectural criticism. My experience is that the public loves it, but architects, editors, developers, advertisers, magazines and newspapers often do not. This makes for some critical conundrums.

Architectural criticism is an art form that many of us would wish to flourish, but it has proven difficult to establish in most places other than a handful of metropoles. The practice of architectural criticism rose in consort with the increasing popularity of newspapers in European then American large cities, then in topical magazines published in the same places. In the English language, our contemporary culture of architectural criticism has its historical roots in the writings of two eminent Victorians: William Morris and John Ruskin.

From William Morris – especially his writings on the preservation of historic buildings – we have inherited the idea of the architecture critic as activist. His writings on buildings were calls to immediate action, and Morris as critic was most effective in describing how layers of historic building details were pulled away in the romantic zeal to restore buildings to one point in their diverse histories. Passing over the line from activist writing to activist organising, Morris then went on to found the preservation lobby group "Anti-Scrape" to carry on the cause. The architectural criticism of urbanist Jane Jacobs and former *New York Times* critic Ada Louise Huxtable are continuations of Morris's notion of invective prose aimed at resolving immediate issues.

Two books by John Ruskin established a related but separate tendency: the architecture critic as moralist. *The Stones of Venice* and, even more so, *The Seven Lamps of Architecture* have a strong foundation in Ruskin's fundamentalist, Calvinist Christian faith. Many of Ruskin's ideas like "truth in structure" and "honesty in materials" became foundational concepts for the Modern movement in architecture, so pervasive now that we forget they had their provenance in Ruskin's paradigm of the Gothic – especially the Italian Gothic he found in Venice and Milan – as the most profound of all the styles. Ruskin's architectural criticism combines muscular descriptive passages with deft interpretation of the moral, even spiritual, implications of architectural decisions. The moralising tendency in architectural criticism was continued in Lewis Mumford's "The Skyline" column for the *New Yorker* magazine, and in the editorship and writing of Peter Davey in his many years at the helm of *The Architectural Review* of London.

To these two streams from the English-language literature of architecture must be added a third one originating in nineteenth-century German philosophy and art historical writing. German-language philosophers from Immanuel Kant and Georg Wilhelm Friedrich Hegel in the nineteenth century to Martin Heidegger and even Ludwig Wittgenstein in the early twentieth century produced theoretical texts and lyrical writings important to our current notions of interpreting and evaluating buildings. In parallel was the German tradition of art historical scholarship demonstrated in the writings of Gottfried Semper during the nineteenth century, Rudolf Wittkower during the twentieth century, and many others. The conflux of these tendencies made for architectural criticism that validated architecture as an intellectually autonomous discipline, disengaging writing from the moralising and strategic concerns of the Morris-Ruskin tradition. At its best, this writing is conceptually rigorous and un-beholden to the distractions of the time and place of its creation, but at its worst it can be pretentious philosophising or pointless formal analysis.

This tendency lives on to this day in that narrow band of architectural criticism as practised by architectural academics and curators, and which is usually – and inaccurately – called 'architectural theory'. The early and mid-career critical practice of Philip Johnson was formalist in character and eclectic in its intellectual borrowings, a combination continued more recently by architect and writer Peter Eisenman and Netherlands Architecture Institute director Aaron Betsky. It is important to note here that there is little place in contemporary academe for the Morris-Ruskin tradition, and indeed for any active practice of architectural criticism that is evaluative and deals with contemporary buildings. On the other hand, that strain of architectural criticism that calls itself 'theory' is carried on only in universities and art galleries, rarely affecting the actual design of buildings or the physical evolution of cities. This separation is itself a serious conundrum; one of my personal hopes for architectural criticism has always been for a reconciliation of these two tendencies.

Through the twentieth century, these traditions of criticism – with linked developments in the French, Italian and Spanish-language architectural press – spread to non-Western countries. As architects in these parts of the world went through the paroxysms of modernisation, there was nearly always a debate about the conflict between tradition and contemporary technology, and another about national identity versus universal ideas and forms. Japan and Latin America first explored these debates in the early twentieth century, followed soon by the rest of Asia, the Middle East and Africa. The new freedoms for the quotation of historical traditions in the Postmodern architecture of the 1980s sparked renewed critical debates in all of these regions, and these discussions evolved simultaneously with those in Euro-American architectural culture. For example, the references to vernacular and religious building forms in the buildings from that period designed by Egyptian architect Abdel Wahed El-Wakil prompted a very interesting debate in the Arab world, one which contains elements from all of the traditions of architectural criticism described above. Yet another conundrum of architectural criticism is that some of the most important debates in architectural culture have occurred away from Western media and academic centres, and have inevitably been seriously under-regarded.

Public criticism is fundamental to architectural culture, but its current precariousness has its roots in how architects are trained. More than any other art, science, or profession, public criticism is an integral part of the education of architects everywhere. As a preface to this phenomenon, it should be noted that the very idea of schools of architecture – rather than master and apprentice systems more typical of the building trades worldwide – is a surprisingly recent invention. Independent schools of architecture with their own pedagogies appeared less than two hundred years ago, with the École des Beaux-Arts in Paris and a London gentleman's club whose evening lectures evolved into a teaching institution, the Architectural Association (AA). For both the Beaux-Arts and the AA, public criticism of student design work became a fundamental technique of architectural education. Engineers, doctors, and even urban planners have nothing like this emphasis on public criticism, and today, open 'crits' or 'reviews' are a component of virtually all the world's architecture schools. While architecture schools carry on regional traditions, and the emphasis in teaching varies from pragmatic building issues to formal and intellectual ambitions, architecture school reviews are nonetheless remarkably similar all around the world. I know this from having participated in reviews of student projects in Sharjah and Jogjakarta, Leuven and Los Angeles, Hong Kong and Halifax. Globally, architects everywhere have their view of the profession and buildings shaped by the particular dynamic of public criticism having been given so prominent a place in their education.

Yet despite this – more likely because of it – critical comments that would hardly generate a murmur if applied to an actor's performance or the assumptions of a scientific brief precipitate shocked and appalled reactions from deeply offended practising architects. Because I have written critical texts in newspapers and magazines about many other art forms and professions, the thin hides of architects have always surprised me. Perhaps I should not be shocked, because when architects lash out at criticism, there often seems to be a deeper psychological dimension to their protests. This is one of the conundrums of our field: the extensive use of architectural criticism as a teaching technique engenders a lifelong dislike of public debate and dialogue amongst too many practising architects. Again, they love the idea of criticism, but not its practice.

The saddest aspect of this particular conundrum is that so much of what is said in architecture schools crits is not actually architectural criticism as I understand it – the interpretation of the intellectual, tectonic, technical and social notions implicit in the designs of buildings and cities – but other types of verbal performance, often tangentially related to the student designs under consideration. The long list of the nonsense that gets spoken in the course of architecture school reviews these days starts, but does not end, with this list: big ego showboating; faux-intellectual fad-gadgetry borrowed from literary theory and cultural studies; private language idolatry by studio gurus; and the Masonic lingo invoked in the socialisation into the architectural profession. I suspect many architects would react better to public criticism had they received a higher level and more focused critical commentary as students.

Criticism of any kind is extraordinarily difficult, requiring high level writing and rhetorical skills. Architectural criticism is perhaps the most difficult of all, because of the range and kinds of knowledge needed to do it, but even more so, because of the very importance of buildings and urban forms in shaping our lives. Architecture critics are like our colleagues in conventional practice – we find it takes up to the age of fifty to develop the writerly and conceptual skills to practise our art with grace and effectiveness. The saddest conundrum of all is that we have fewer and fewer places to publish considered architectural criticism every year.

Because the public criticism of buildings is so difficult, dangerous and debt-inducing, the numbers of practising critics are tiny. For example, all of us who live by writing on buildings in Canada can ride together in a taxi, and the International Committee of Architectural Critics (CICA) – the global architecture critics' organisation – has 120 members. I have no doubt that there are rare subspecies of Himalayan moulds or Arctic sea slugs that rate more specialists looking at them than does commentary and exegesis on contemporary construction. Following a pattern in many other cities, the post of architecture critic was abolished at both daily newspapers in Seattle within one month of each other last year. This loss of a public forum happened after a reported campaign by the development industry to eliminate those irksome independent opinions – builders want solely their weekend 'homes pages' advertorial coverage. Not only our designers want to control architectural criticism, it seems.

My city of Vancouver has one of the most dynamic and interesting building cultures on the continent, but the main daily newspaper here recently cut architectural criticism from once monthly to none at all, meaning that the entire north-west quadrant of North America is now without any independent specialist commentary on architecture in its daily newspapers. This is one of the cruellest conundrums of all: for one of the most public of the arts of appreciation, there are fewer and fewer places to practise it. While local critical coverage has diminished, we have seen more and more coverage about fewer and fewer global architects, and the coverage has shifted from true criticism to celebrity journalism. Celebrity coverage of 'starchitects' and their latest sculptings have displaced criticism and commentary on buildings and cities in most mainstream periodicals.

The situation in magazines is only marginally better. Amongst the 'glossies', the highest profile international English-language architecture magazines, only London's *The Architectural Review* maintains a regular commitment to criticism, as opposed to the descriptive and explanatory writing more common to design journals. While Toronto's *Canadian Architect* and New York's *Architectural Record* occasionally publish pointed criticism, critical writing is not a high priority amongst the information conglomerate corporations that own them, no matter what the personal priorities of their editors. Urban magazines such as *Metropolis* and *Blueprint* do slightly better, but even the best of shelter magazines – such as the otherwise clever *Dwell* magazine – promote a kind of cheerleading promotional writing that is only occasionally, maybe even accidentally, critical.

The new frontiers of architectural criticism are all electronic. For Radio France, François Chaslin has demonstrated how effective architecture can be in the aural space of a sound-only medium. Feature films by Louis Kahn's son and about Antoni Gaudí demonstrate how effective the high resolution, large image of the cinema can be when it turns its sights on the built environment, and upon the creative minds who shape buildings and cities. There is much hope that the Internet will provide the forum so needed for architectural criticism. I find that my articles published in newspapers and magazines now have a lively after-life, as they are picked up and commented on by information hubs such as www.archnewsnow.com, then in commentary in blogs and specialist websites. The critical conundrum here is that these new places for commentary are important, but by definition they are diffuse, lacking the impact and import of ideas applied to local issues in a public way. As architecture critics, we are developing global publics, but are less and less able, in the William Morris manner, to shape events and build culture close to home.

Television has blown hot and cold about architecture over the years. Programmes about domestic design and house 'makeovers' have never been more popular than now, and there is a rudimentary form of criticism at play in these reality programmes. CNN and other news networks have featured weekly shows about design culture, but they took a deadly turn towards the coverage of design stars, and, frankly, compared to movie and music-makers, even our most famous architects are just not that interesting as personalities.

The Qatar-based news network Aljazeera has just spent one billion dollars launching a new global English-language service. Those of us privileged to visit, teach and occasionally write about architecture in the Middle East know that there is a huge interest in Western countries about the evolution of cities there, especially in the Gulf region. The issues are global, and the stakes are high as cities here transform themselves month by month. Will Kuwait City set a separate course from the extravagance and schmaltz of much of Dubai's tourist-oriented development? Has the condominium apartment turned into a global commodity, to be traded across borders like crude oil or orange juice futures, or does housing still have some relation to the cities in which it is plunked down? Riyadh, Ankara and

Damascus have enormous issues of urban infrastructure, but also enormous reserves of talent and ideas to deal with them. I hope an enlightened Aljazeera producer finds time in their news programme for a show about design and cities. I suspect it would be surprisingly popular on the English-language network, and even more so on the Arabic one. The world will be watching.

The website referenced in this essay was accessed in May 2006.

Frames of Reference for Architectural Criticism

ALI CENGIZKAN

Where the nature of architectural criticism is discussed with regard to its implications, attitudes to it, and its relation to architectural journalism, I find it timely to search for ways to revise our academic understanding of it. As Hani Rashid mentioned in his paper presented at this meeting, the cultural diversity of architectural criticism and journalism is a striking global issue, where the objectivity and subjectivity of criticism may be mentioned and also articulated with diverse levels of intuitive, opinionated and promotional approaches, but with all these dimensions operating as a field constituting a common denominator to all professionals in the discipline. However, the term 'architectural criticism' still relates to an endeavour belonging to an academic field of thinking, where canons of historiography are continuously operating, setting the values and value judgements towards the legitimacy of a new object of art, in this case, architecture.[1] Although the canons themselves are open to inquiry, especially at times of crisis, it is usual that the consensus on the dominating paradigm in the field creates a perpetual production and reproduction of the basic positions in that field, leading to a status quo.

When making its statements, architectural criticism has the possibilities to claim social, cultural, aesthetic, economic, historiographic, political and similar engagements to positions located within the profession as well as in neighbouring fields and disciplines. Not only do these signify the reality of the very position of the architectural critic, they also act as frames of reference in the making of architectural criticism. Architecture, as a collective practice with a functional aim, has to account to public opinion at different levels and at different times, regardless of whether the public is the professional community, the small administrative group, the user association, the anonymous customer, or the citizens of a city at large.

Why is this so? I would like to start the discussion with Hani Rashid's remarks made in this meeting regarding Modern architecture, which expressed concern about its "inflated promises, so rampant in the mid to late twentieth century, [which] had resulted only in a failure, especially with respect to locality and difference". Architectural criticism is always bound to the current meta-narratives in the discipline of architecture, namely the discursive field, which tend to guide its practice and its self-positioning processes through criticism and historiography(ies), where canons are shared by the audience, including the practitioners, academicians, users and patrons.

It is more understandable and easier to decipher now how the earth has become a uniform place, or a collection of uniform places. This has occurred as a result of the rapid processes and mechanisms of globalisation, which 'Modernity' unceasingly called for with its praise for the 'universal human being', and with its will for 'the rational' in an endeavour to attain anonymous global terrain and to maintain a uniform global culture out of diverse cultures. This objective was achieved through the unaccountable struggles of anonymous subjects, with the help of the hidden language of the discourses of successive developments towards the positivistic comprehension of welfare society.

I would argue that, among other things, Modern architecture itself is a discursive field, a mental state of mind, set for general consensus with regard to an ideological position with its relevant moral values. This mental state of mind is closely related to rationalism, giving rationality priority in all issues, and reducing experience and experientiality to a secondary level. However, this rationalism is closely related to positivism as well, rooted in common grounds that are taken for granted, where both rationalism and positivism claim that the world is a place that is knowable and controllable.

I presume that the debate between the positions of 'situated' avant-gardes and their positions regarding their early and late experiments with buildings is a result of our understanding of their 'Modernness'.[2] We can feel content to have created this vicious circle. Without settling on 'Modern architecture' in these terms, it is hard to grasp current architecture and create its criticism. Thus, opposing 'Modern architecture' as a style, but treating it through stylistic components when criticism and historiography are concerned, is a common and shared state of cognitive dissonance.

Without getting settled into this definition and coming to terms with it, architectural criticism continues to be situated under the prerogative of Modernism as a movement. Criticism acts not to criticise, but to promote and even legitimise 'situated knowledge' about Modernism. This vicious circle contends quite a number of people in the field of architecture: practitioners, theoreticians, academicians and historiographers, all of whom are at ease regarding the safe though shattered grounds of the present. By taking/reducing the issue of Modernism to a choice about style, whether objective, subjective, intuitive, opinionated, or promotional, positions may be picked up as free options and as legitimate choices in the field of criticism.

So the question of an audience for architectural criticism is solved to a certain degree: the players in the field, regardless of their origin and role, are complying with existing rules and norms. They 'buy and sell what they ask for' (as a metaphor to stock-exchange dealers); they are indifferent to that with which they are unfamiliar; and they are only open to guidance by the popular mass media in reshaping their tastes, arguments and positions. So how can the audience at large be reshaped?

Here the current roles and tasks required of current architectural criticism emerge: it should be highly critical of every contemporary phenomenon, and of new objects, concepts and statements in this highly globalised and diversified field of practice. However, as the example below reminds us, it should also demand the unifying of architectural criticism into an entity that not only indulges diverse interests in a multidisciplinary way, but also presents a consistent, self-reflexive and self-constructive body of knowledge to clear its way out of this vicious circle, towards a more self-critical field. To achieve this, new frames of reference should be proposed, discussed and set out.

EXEMPLAR: DUBAI TOWERS IN ISTANBUL

During the past decade in Turkey, actors from the global market have been invited to invest in urban real estate projects. In 2005, the Municipality of Metropolitan Istanbul decided to enter into a partnership arrangement with one of these investors, Dubai International Properties, to develop high-rise towers in one of the city's districts. A huge programme of investment that aimed at reaching five billion USD in five years was launched for this project without seeking the prior consent of the city's citizens.

The proposed project, the Dubai Towers, was to be located in Levent, a crowded, newly flourishing area of the city that is emerging as the new central business district, which is already being disabled as a result of several problems affecting it. As municipal property, not only did the area earmarked for the project consist of public land to which the public has a claim, but the enterprise, with its 300-metre-high towers, would also modify the skyline of the city. Public debate and resistance regarding the project, reflected in the mass media, particularly in newspapers and television, proved to be an active initiative, more so than the promotional campaign that the project investor launched. However, the weakest party proved to be the architects. They considered the possibility/impossibility of the high-rise, its legitimacy as a work of architectural design, and whether the building design proposal had a real layout, with a sound level of creativity, rather than being a utopian example of paper architecture compared with other proposals. But with this very act, architects could easily be blamed as the ones who offered legitimacy to this object of 'corporate architecture'.[3]

REFLECTIONS ON THE MEDIA

As evident in the cartoon images and news about the project highlighted in the press, the popular media proved to be actively responsive towards this architectural intervention, not only in regard to the final object, but also to the decision-making process involved, including the handling of public concerns, the planning projections and constructs created, the political judgements made, the social inclusion/exclusion it engendered, the degree of governance and objective decision-making concerned, and the range of social responsibility felt for the public interest. The diversity expressed in these news items and cartoons is highly significant, and shows sensitivity towards an urban issue created in the hands of architectural practice (see figs. 1–16).

Fig. 1. "We are not planning
a 650-metre-tall skyscraper". The Mayor
of Istanbul, *Hürriyet*, 9.10.2005.

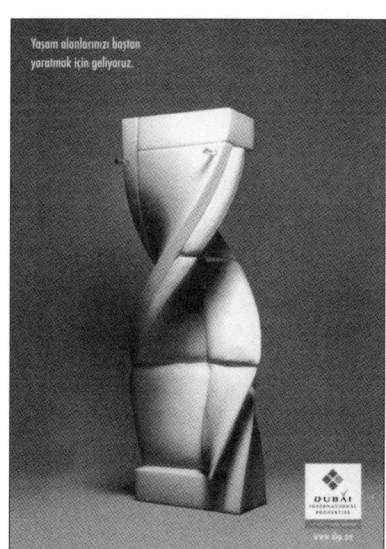

Fig. 2. "We are coming to recreate
your living environments."
A Dubai International Properties public
relations leaflet for the project, 1.11.2005.

Fig. 3. "Here is Dubai Towers-Istanbul.
As one of the best examples of modern
architecture, the Dubai Towers will rise
to the sky in Istanbul, in the 'capital' of the
Turkish business sphere [...] It will have
a five-star hotel, office spaces equipped
with high technology, intelligent housing
units..." A Dubai International Properties
public relations leaflet for the project,
1.11.2005.

Fig. 4. Prejudice vs. Pellucidity.
"Principle of Transparency?"
"Don't worry about that!
We will make the skyscraper transparent!",
Behiç Ak, *Cumhuriyet*, 26.10.2005.

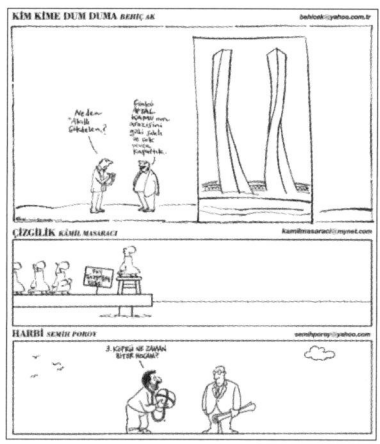

Fig. 5. Public Wisdom vs.
Private Deviations. "Why the Intelligent
Skyscraper?" "Because we fooled the public,
by using public land at no cost",
Behiç Ak, *Cumhuriyet*, 27.10.2005.

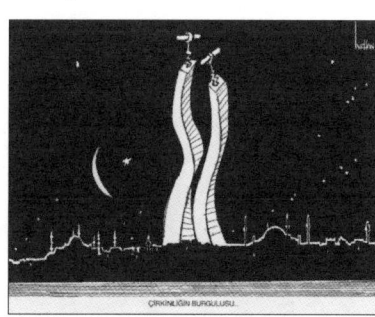

Fig. 6. Urban Threat Dooming
Sociocultural Peace. "The Disgusting
Cork-Screw", Turhan Selçuk,
Cumhuriyet, 27.10.2005.

Fig. 7. Professional Enjoyment.
"Dubai Towers in 10 Questions
and Answers", Ali Müfit Gürtuna
and Ahmet Vefik Alp, *Aktüel*, 1.11.2005.

şehir

BU DA NEYİN NESİ DİYENLERE
10 SORUDA DUBAİ KULELERİ

Son günlerin tartışması İstanbul'da yapılması planlanan Dubai gökdelen projesi. Akla takılan soruları eski İstanbul Belediye Başkanı Ali Müfit Gürtuna ve Yüksek Mimar Ahmet Vefik Alp yanıtladı.

Fig. 8. A New Metaphor Is Born.
"The idea comes from
the Whirling Dervish!",
an anonymous journalist,
Hürriyet, 13.11.2005.

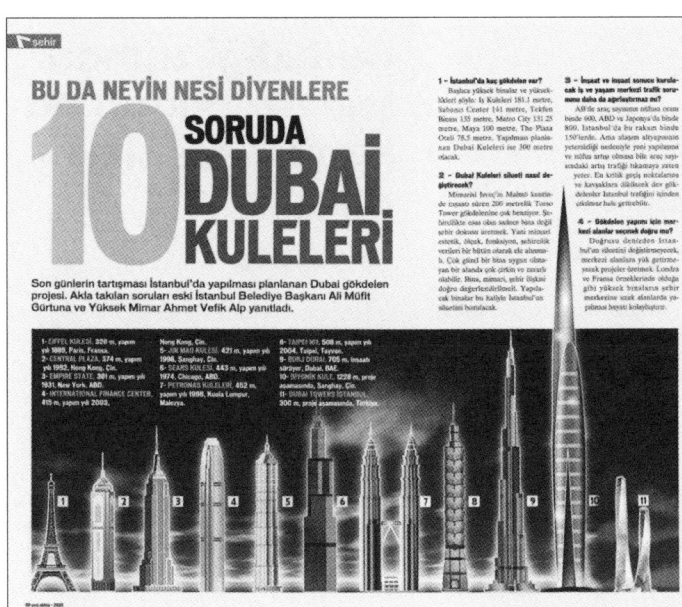

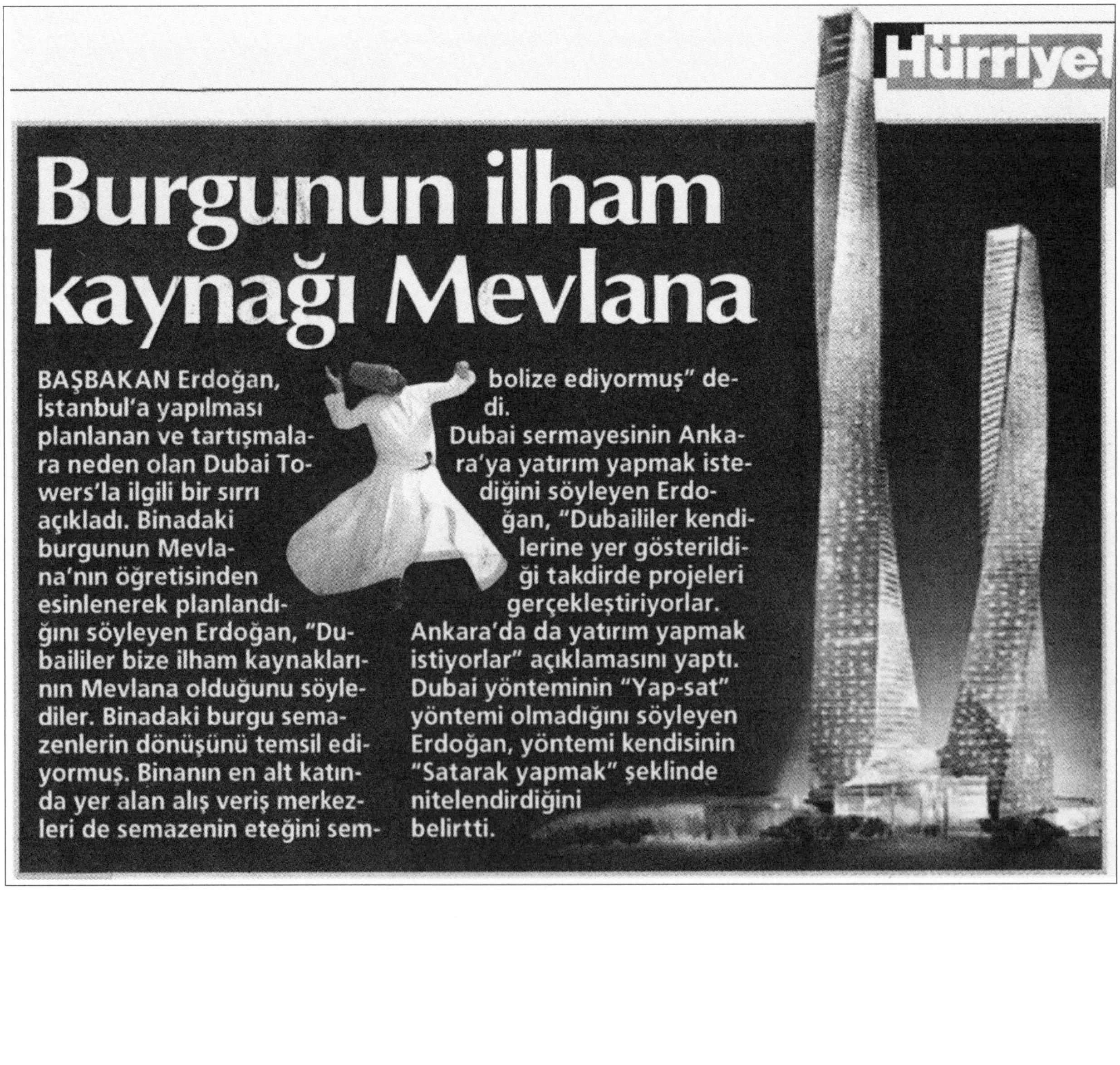

Hürriyet

Burgunun ilham kaynağı Mevlana

BAŞBAKAN Erdoğan, İstanbul'a yapılması planlanan ve tartışmalara neden olan Dubai Towers'la ilgili bir sırrı açıkladı. Binadaki burgunun Mevlana'nın öğretisinden esinlenerek planlandığını söyleyen Erdoğan, "Dubaililer bize ilham kaynaklarının Mevlana olduğunu söylediler. Binadaki burgu semazenlerin dönüşünü temsil ediyormuş. Binanın en alt katında yer alan alış veriş merkezleri de semazenin eteğini sembolize ediyormuş" dedi.

Dubai sermayesinin Ankara'ya yatırım yapmak istediğini söyleyen Erdoğan, "Dubaililer kendilerine yer gösterildiği takdirde projeleri gerçekleştiriyorlar. Ankara'da da yatırım yapmak istiyorlar" açıklamasını yaptı. Dubai yönteminin "Yap-sat" yöntemi olmadığını söyleyen Erdoğan, yöntemi kendisinin "Satarak yapmak" şeklinde nitelendirdiğini belirtti.

Fig. 9. Concern for Urban
Infrastructure and Public Welfare.
"It is good not to have hurricanes in our
country that upturn cities [while he reads
'Hurricane Wilma has hit Florida']",
Musa Kart, *Cumhuriyet*, 13.11.2005.

Levent-Çeliktepe'den Dubai Towers

Fig. 10. Concern for Politics of Space.
"Dubai Towers and the Revolt of the
Turkish Varosha, or Parisienne Banlieu."
"The existing modernist neighbourhood
will be the junkyard", Haydar Karabey,
Radikal İki, 13.11.2005.

**Dubai gökdelenleri hem İstanbul'un kimliğini bo-
zacak hem de altyapı sorunlarını katlayacak.**

Mimarlar ve şehir plancıları

'Yatırım değil şımarıklık abideleri'

TMMOB Mimarlar Odası Genel Başkanı
Ekinci, Dubai sermayesinin tasarladığı
ikiz kulelerin, "sonradan görme bir zen-
ginliğin yarattığı şımarıklık abideleri" olduğunu söyledi. SHP İstanbul İl Başkanı
Özkahraman, Türkiye'nin yabancı serma-
yeye peşkeş çekildiğini ve projelerin istih-
dama dönük olmadığını vurguladı.

Şehir Plancıları Odası İstanbul Şube Sekre-
teri Nurhan, bölgenin zaten altyapı ve ula-
şım konularında çok sayıda sorunu bulun-
duğunu belirterek "Gökdelenler yapılın-
ca bölgenin sorunlarının halledilmesi için
yeni yatırımlar yapılması gerekecek. Yani
bu para halkın cebinden çıkacak" dedi.
GÖKÇE UYGUN'un haberi ■ *6. Sayfada*

Fig. 11a, b (left and top). Chambers
of Architects and Engineers criticise:
"Not Investments but Monuments
of Arrogance", an anonymous journalist,
Cumhuriyet, 26.10.2005.

Fig. 12. Concern for Politics of Space;
Preservation. "'The highest' form of kitsch:
Istanbul as the World Heritage in the hands
of the newly-rich", Oktay Ekinci,
Cumhuriyet, 27.10.2005.

Fig. 13. Concern for Politics of Space and Global Politics. "A great burden for Turkey: They will return even richer", Necdet Çalışkan, *Cumhuriyet*, 28.10.2005.

Fig. 14. Concern for National and Domestic Politics. "Here is our source of inspiration. He became Prime Minister after several turns", Musa Kart, *Cumhuriyet*, 28.10.2005.

Fig. 15. Concern for Urban Land and Infrastructure. "Levent as a district cannot support these towers!", an anonymous journalist, *Radikal*, 30.10.2005.

Figs. 16a, b. Concern for Similar Enterprises of the Authorities:
• Privatisation of the port of Galata
• Privatisation of the Haydarpafla railway station
• The new shopping malls
These were recent attempts by the authorities (both central and local) to carry out extensive urban renewal projects on publicly-owned land through overturning and disregarding legitimate procedures, an anonymous journalist, *Cumhuriyet* (21.9.2005) and *Cumhuriyet Pazar* and *Radikal İki* (23.10.2005) respectively.

CONCLUSION

It would seem that the counter-argument to a public structure the size of the Dubai Towers and its impact indicates that architectural interrogation should not be developed as a matter of architectural style, as a problem of anti-aesthetics, as a case of nationalistic and professional, but inevitably territorial, defence, or as an object of national attack perpetuated with pride and a sense of offence. It is not that all these positions lack valid reasoning and strength, but that their overall validity and power rest on the total impact of collective action, taken as a message and given as a discursive end product. What is critical may not be supported by any of these arguments, and architects may prove to be one of the weakest groups in developing a sound position on such a project, missing the diverse nature of the problem, as well as lacking converging arguments. As a result, this case in Turkey shows that the bombardments in the media by caricaturists, columnists, non-governmental organisations, community activists, civic service representatives and even architects and engineers against the project and its public relations campaign proved to be successful. As a result, the project has been halted and is awaiting public approval. Some believe that time will encourage people to think and pave the way for reconciliations, in a settling of diverse ideas; others are looking for the right moment to act.

Architectural criticism, by definition, has to consider diverse criteria from social, cultural, aesthetic, economic, historiographic and political spheres, and has to regard relevant theoretical positions as frames of reference when making its statements. Architecture, as a collective practice with a functional aim, has to account for public opinion at different levels and at different times. The public may be the professional community, the administrative group, the user association, the anonymous customers, or the citizens of a city at large. The production of architectural criticism as a self-reflexive activity must enhance self-criticism as well as criticism of its very objects and targets. Architectural criticism should develop its own targets in order to read, promote, accentuate, clarify, rectify and decipher objects of architecture. It is a subjective endeavour in its origin, and, by the same token, a creative process.

[1] For conceiving and understanding historical (as well as architectural) values for works of architecture, the timeless text by nineteenth-century art historian Alois Riegl remains unsurpassed. See Alois Riegl, "The Modern Cult of Monuments: Its Character and Its Origin", in *Oppositions, A Journal for Ideas and Criticism in Architecture*, 25, autumn 1982, pp. 20–51.

[2] For a well-articulated recent account of this topic, see Sarah Williams Goldhagen, "Something to Talk About: Modernism, Discourse, Style", in *Journal of the Society of Architectural Historians*, 64: 2, June 2005, pp. 144–167.

[3] It is also revealing that the designers for the project came from abroad. This shows that there is a lack of architectural design capacity in Turkey that has the capabilities to parallel and compete with the "Global Intelligence Corps" as labelled and defined by Anthony King. See Anthony D. King, *Spaces of Global Cultures: Architecture, Urbanism, Identity*, Routledge Architext Series, Taylor and Francis, London 2004, p. 21.

Architectural Form and the 'Spirit of the Age'

HUSSAIN MOUSA DASHTI

At the beginning of any architectural design process, all that an architect has is a design programme, raw data relating to the design problem and some preliminary assumptions. The architect then starts making freehand sketches, manipulating lines and shapes using some computer-aided design (CAD) programs, or building study models. After a long process of form exploration and design development, a certain form for the building being designed evolves.

The generation of a formal concept is obviously central to the design of buildings, and the creation of forms is a key issue that lies at the heart of the profession of architecture. I have always wondered about the sources of architectural form. I have wanted to know what runs through the minds of architects when faced with design challenges. Do architects first study the design programme and its requirements and try to tackle the design problem from a functional perspective? Or do they manipulate lines and shapes to create a geometric system that appeals to them, and that they may adopt for their buildings? Do they have certain intuitive ideas that they express in forms? How do architects think about the forms they create?

During this critical stage of creating something from scratch, architects intuitively have sought a set of normative theories for guiding their activities. The search for sources of building forms is not limited to architectural practice, but is a central issue to theories in other fields, ranging from art to anthropology. Although these fields are not concerned with creating building forms, practitioners in such fields examine building forms to explain certain social or cultural phenomena.

There are some important theories that have been used to interpret architectural form. Some of these theories are intuitive, others are pragmatic, and others are computational. Each of these theories has its merits and shortcomings.

In the pragmatic category, form-related theories include, but are not limited to, the theory "form follows function". This theory, which was coined by the American architect Louis Sullivan during the late nineteenth century, links the form of the building to its intended purpose. It is a theory associated with Modern architecture. Theories that deal with the impact of physical conditions, such as construction methods, building technology and materials, site, and so on, on architectural form may also be placed under the same category.

In the intuitive category, one may include theories that view architectural form as a way of expression, communication and symbolism, as well as theories that establish a link between architectural identity and form. Also under this category comes the theory addressing form as being generated by the imagination of the designer's 'genius'.

Theories in the computational category, which are the most recent, are changing the way architectural forms appear. During the past decade, digital media have been used increasingly as generative tools for the derivation and transformation of complicated forms that had never been thought of before. Computational form-related theories include digital derivatives of a master geometry, "digital morphogenesis" and "generative architectural form". Here, digitally-generated forms are calculated by generative processes. Instead of creating an external form, architects create an internal generative logic, which can then be used to automatically produce a wide range of form possibilities from which an architect may select a form to develop. "Performative architecture" and building form is another relevant theory in which a building is defined not by the way it looks, but by the way it performs, that is, by its impact on culture and the way it transforms culture. Architectural form and digitally-driven building fabrication is another relevant computational theory.

I presume that architectural form is a result of the prevailing spirit of the age and place. Each place in a specific period or age possesses a certain 'spirit' derived from a set of shared attitudes and trends that give the architectural creation of the place a more or less typical quality and character. Despite the attempts of architects to exhibit individual characteristics derived from their own philosophies, their work will unconsciously respond to common views, tastes and artistic values they inevitably share with each other. These shared views and values are often published in architectural journals. While some architects are very eager to publish in such journals, others do not publish, but are highly influenced by what critics publish about their works or about the works of other architects. Architects definitely are either directly or indirectly influenced by the different directions of architectural criticism, particularly formalist criticism. Therefore, criticism is another issue to be added to my extensive list as I search for sources of architectural form.

Fog in the Desert

LUIS FERNÁNDEZ-GALIANO

We do not expect fog in the desert. Nevertheless, we Western critics and our counterparts from the Muslim world who have been summoned together in Kuwait by the Aga Khan Award for Architecture were met by extraordinary weather conditions, by a mist that is denser than the mythical British split-pea soup. This fog is so unusual that it makes the front page of the *Arab Times*, Kuwait's English-language daily. It blurs the silhouette of the city's architectural icon, the Kuwait Towers, a construction of water tanks that also serves as a lookout and restaurants. While dining in one of the towers, it occurs to me that the fog inside which we are conversing is a perfect metaphor for the soft, cottony blindness of the world's privileges. After all, as we savour desserts flown in that same morning from a Parisian patisserie, we are floating many metres above the dunes that hide the lake of petroleum on whose viscous darkness rests the prosperity of the Gulf, but also ours.

The Kuwaitis follow the news of Saddam Hussein's trial with indifference. Gone, almost entirely, are the marks of the invasion that in 1990 provoked the first Gulf War – with unforeseen architectural consequences in Spain, such as the interruption of the construction in Madrid of the 1996 Puerta de Europa twin towers, which were built by the Kuwait Investments Office, or the celebration of victory over Iraq through the lyrical Kuwaiti Pavilion at Expo '92 in Seville, which Santiago Calatrava designed as an arch of triumph of moving palm trees. One hardly remembers that the geopolitical balance of the planet still rests on this fragile hinge where energy reserves intersect with the clash of civilisations. During these pre-Christmas weeks, passenger planes fly fearlessly over a shaken, pre-electoral Iraq, and in Kuwait, people worry more about highway traffic jams than about metal detector arches or the routine checking of the undersides and trunks of vehicles at the entrances to hotels.

The parliament building designed by Jørn Utzon, with its huge canvases of concrete hanging from the sculptural portico, continues to be the country's most beautiful building. It has been entirely restored to what it was like before the 1990 Iraqi occupation, when it suffered considerable damage. At the same time, new skyscrapers built in corporate styles are sprouting left and right, alongside shopping centres with a Californian air and incomparable luxuries. If we pass through the real estate fair that accompanies an ongoing congress of local engineers, we cannot help but think that

Kuwait is preparing to become another Dubai, the Gulf emirate currently second only to Shanghai in number of cranes.

Contemplating this Persian or Arabian Gulf on whose fortune our own so much depends, the year's architectural events fade in the blue fog of distance and in the indifference of chance. The cities of the year were Aichi, site of an International Exposition of environmental sustainability themes that accommodated a much praised Spanish Pavilion: a ceramic and chromatic work by Alejandro Zaera and Farshid Moussavi; Istanbul, venue of a congress of the International Union of Architects (UIA) that awarded its triennial medal to the Japanese architect Tadao Ando; and London, elected host of the Olympic Games of 2012, beating Paris, Madrid, New York and Moscow the day before being the target of a chain of terrorist attacks. However, for a year that began under the tragic effects of a tsunami that claimed a quarter of a million victims, perhaps the list of cities ought to include New Orleans, dramatically devastated by Hurricane Katrina; Paris, scene of the decade's worst urban disturbances; and Madrid, which saw the Windsor office tower burn and made us realise how vulnerable the vertical city is. This roster of disasters will soon include Tokyo, a privileged hub of fashion architectures like Toyo Ito's Tod's or SANAA's Dior, but today also the epicentre of a political and technical scandal that threatens to cut short Japan's economic recovery after revelations of architect Hidetsugu Aneha's falsification of seismic calculations in order to reduce construction costs in over fifty buildings, which will now have to be demolished. Experts say that this problem, which results from the complicity of architects, builders and inspectors (often belonging to private companies since the construction sector has been liberalised), could affect tens of thousands of constructions in the country.

Incidentally, this was one of the issues addressed at the Kuwait gathering because it affects that essential factor of security and life without which it is obscene to be lavish in aesthetic considerations, considerations that are perhaps reasonably limited to the lazaretto of culture supplements in newspapers, which cannot compete with the juicy polemics of the local news section, the exotic proposals of the travel pages, or the sophisticated lifestyle coverage of Sunday magazines, not to mention the endless advertising of real estate sections. After all, it is reasonable to think that the urbanistic mutations of one's own city, the architectural glamour of tourist destinations, or domestic decoration – not to mention the buying of a dwelling, a rite of passage that marks one's stepping from the freedom of youth to the mortgaged chains of maturity –, are all eons more interesting than the often lewd ramblings about the physical body of architecture and its fleeting shadows, an activity of idlers like the critics gathered together in the unexpected mists of the Gulf.

To discipline this tameless tribe, and in the spirit of guiding the reader, let me attempt to finish a short adaptation of a transatlantic doctrine in matters of obscenity, one I extract from the instructions offered by a Virginia-based organisation called Parents Against Bad Books in Schools. The organisation has put together a list of works judged "inappropriate, obscene, or vulgar", including works by the likes of Umberto Eco, Margaret Atwood and Gabriel García Márquez.[1] According to *The Times Literary Supplement* (TLS), the 'badness' of texts is measured by a scale of four registers having to do with sexual content that move from B (Basic) to G (Graphic), on to VG (Very Graphic) and EG (Extremely Graphic). Examples are given: B (large breasts); G (large, voluptuous bouncing breasts); VG (large, voluptuous bouncing breasts with hard nipples); EG (large, voluptuous bouncing breasts with hard nipples covered with glistening sweat and bite marks).[2] An equivalent architectural scale to prevent critical pornography could go as follows: B (large volumes); G (large, undulating and agitated volumes); VG (large, undulating and agitated volumes clad with titanium): EG (large, undulating and agitated volumes clad with titanium, with a moist gloss and trembling texture). Such a scale could serve as a guide for architectural critics lost in the fog of exclusive sensuality while the dark pulse of the world beats beneath the sand.

The website referenced in this essay was accessed in May 2006.

---

[1] See the web site of Parents Against Bad Books in Schools (PABBIS) at www.pabbis.com/bookreview.html.

[2] This discussion appeared in an editorial commentary by J. C. in *The Times Literary Supplement*, 5338 (22 July 2005), 14.

An Approach to Architectural Criticism
LOUISE NOELLE GRAS

The study of art, to which architecture belongs, may be approached in two manners that in a certain way are complementary to each other. On the one hand, there is the process of identification, classification and exhibition, as well as the selling and buying of objects. On the other, there is the rigorous study of objects, which in certain cases may be called criticism: the analysis of the value of a specific work.

In this sense, the formulation of a judgement cannot be totally objective, but it should never be a synonym for condemnation. Its true purpose is the analysis, explanation and appreciation of architectural work. It should be added that architecture allows diverse criteria of analysis and evaluation that depend on the person who carries out the criticism, as well as on the intended receptor. The point of view of a scholar will be presented in a different manner when intended for fellow academicians than when intended for the general public; it will also be presented differently if it targets the architect of a project. In this latter case, it would be useful to include the architect's own reflections on his or her own work, which is a type of self-criticism that pertains to an important process of learning.

It is indispensable that a serious analysis examines a building from different perspectives. This type of study is based on knowledge. Besides researching the building, the critic should visit and examine the work in question. Furthermore, it is important to note that beneath the umbrella of architecture, we may find different disciplines that involve the building individually or collectively, such as urbanism, landscape architecture, interior design, restoration and rehabilitation. All of these also reach the realms of diverse specialisations in fields including structure, acoustics, optics and lighting.

In criticism, the historical and geographic contexts should be taken into consideration, in the same way that the impact of the building on its surroundings and its links with the environment should be addressed. The critic should evaluate the exterior composition of the building as well as the ensuing spatial results in the interior; all of this within the context of the functional requirements of each building and its final intended use. The analysis should also pay attention to technological and structural problems and challenges, as well as to the construction materials and techniques used, taking into account the economic considerations of the solutions. The work of criticism should be informed about the social context, evaluating the cultural surroundings of place and time. Finally, it is necessary to take into account the architect and his or her professional career, and to assess the architect's creative contributions within a specific project.

This long list of issues demonstrates the richness and multiplicity of the architectural endeavour, from which arises a considerable difficulty in carrying out accessible written works. In fact, a thorough or exhaustive discourse on all these points, even if it has the advantage of getting as close as possible to complete objectivity, may become too long and tedious for the reader. At this point, the 'talent' of the critic comes into play; the critic can then introduce the subjectivity that allows him or her to choose and highlight the subjects that offer the most interest within the context of a specific building.

To establish credibility, the architectural critic must have an ethical position, basing opinions and analysis on his or her knowledge, without voicing opinions born of ulterior motives. Such knowledge should be related to theoretical proposals. Through anchoring his or her voice to a theoretical framework in a relatively explicit way, the critic presents a consistent and constant discourse, and the reader can identify with what is expressed.

It is fundamental to understand the individual voice of an architectural critic, since it has been established that objectivity cannot be met in the field of criticism. It is therefore important to know about the different authors to better understand their positions. In this sense, critics, especially those who are present in the mass media, can have a huge impact amongst readers as well as architects.

Finally, it may be said that architectural criticism today has become a discipline with a wide array of protagonists, which demonstrates its relevance to overall cultural discourse. A proof of this is the increase in the number of published architectural monographs over the last two decades. However, not all of these publications deserve to belong to the category of 'criticism'. It is also desirable to see an expansion of the production of this type of critical approach in periodicals, as well as in the mass media. This expansion may help solve the problem that French architect Pierre Vago addressed when he stated that "architects see, but do not read". It would be desirable to develop audiovisual products aimed at architects, as well as a broader audience that consists of people who enjoy architectural creations, or at least have to bear with them.

Architecture after the Age of Knowledge

ROMI KHOSLA

I am not very sure which era we are seeing the beginning of. History has been taught to us in packages of 'eras' and 'isms' for so long that I feel completely lost in this day of rapid fast-forward moving events. We can wait for the wise observers of human events to provide us with another lasting label for the decades that lie ahead, or else we can engage in our own speculation in this brief period that is free from labels. There is a small window of opportunity here for us architects.

I am reliably told that we can safely say that self-contained societies and communities are a thing of the past, when history was alive and kicking. Now, there is the inescapable logic of interdependence upon us, brought about by the abundantly available fresh air of globalisation.

But I do not find any of this convincing. I believe that such a state of uncertainty is a permanent feature in our lives. It is in these conditions of uncertainty that we become the most creative. It is indeed the dividing line between uncertainty and certainty that separates the concerns of architects and critics. Architects enjoy the risks of uncertainty. They love the potentials of the fuzzy line that separates the possible from the impossible. Dreaming about, and exploring, the realms of the possible and impossible is heady stuff that is uncertain in its outcome. Perhaps it is the critics who bring us back to earth. For me, it is critics who are the hosts who celebrate architecture. As an architect, I need to indulge in these celebrations. But it is not my loneliness that eggs me on to attend these celebrations and treat them seriously. I have begun to treat them as reality checks to measure whether I am with the world as it moves on, or whether I have lost it and gone gaga. So, one important relationship I have with critics is that of being a guest in their celebrations of architecture, and it is of course important for me whether they include me in these celebrations or not.

However, lately – secretly perhaps – I have been rather happy that the dividing line between practice and criticism has become fuzzy, and consequently a feeling of bondage seems to have lifted. I have begun to celebrate the uncertainty of the times, perhaps because the authoritative foundations of knowledge that lay secure for so long have begun to be shaken by real events. Originally, these foundations were laid in that era that was termed for us the Enlightenment, and it seems to me that all the enlightened social sciences were formulated with such wonderful theories about society.

And armed – as critics were – with this knowledge of how society and therefore architecture ought to be, our work was always celebrated or condemned within the confines of that body of knowledge. As the authority of knowledge is becoming increasingly uncertain, so is the bondage that it wrapped around us even as practising architects. It is almost as if the teacher had left the classroom rather suddenly.

In architecture, what is good and not so good mercifully has become an unknown domain. I use the word 'mercifully' because, for too long, the interpretation of architecture had carried the conscience of the social sciences without admitting that it itself is part of the social experiment that has impacted human, technical, ecological, social and cultural domains. Of course, early Modern architecture carried the enormous weight of these domains in their entirety. However, more recently, during the last three decades or so, architecture seems to have thrown out much of that social baggage and transferred its attention from macro to micro social models. Architecture more and more is being represented and transmuted in mediums that press flat real space into images of that space.

I therefore find uncertainty and confusion mercifully exciting. I dread the prospect of another era, another set of 'isms', or another reformulation of social concepts that could provide architecture with fresh new baggage and a new critical mass of accepted norms, rules and regulations that ensure compliances with some or other 'ism' or ideology. The uncertainty is exciting because it makes space for multiple interpretations, which will need to be carried out from the edge of the field that is architecture. I feel more comfortable regarding architecture as a field rather than an art, a social catalyst, or good engineering. Rather, in this field, all sorts of games are played in all sorts of styles with multiple surface meanings as well as deep ones. To interpret the meanings of what is now occurring in the field, one needs to interpret architecture in multiple ways, in multiple styles, through different mediums, and across the boundaries of cultures that the earlier authority of knowledge had arranged in hierarchies, superiorities and inferiorities.

If the first expectation I as an architect have of critics is to share their celebration of architecture, my second expectation of them is to share a ride with them as they travel the very bumpy road across cultural barriers. The hardest and perhaps the most challenging effort we have to make is to interpret and transmit our perceptions across cultural divides. When architecture or the interpretation of architecture moves across a cultural divide, it addresses by its fresh presence in a culture the potential conflicts and similarities between cultures, and this inevitably brings attention to the problems of negotiations and interpretations.

Let me try and explain this seemingly diffused notion of the interpretation of architecture in the world today. I come from an ancient and wrinkled civilisation full of diffused notions about the nature of human existence. Multiple interpretations and the relativity of phenomena are part of our conditioning. I suspect there could be others in the field of architecture who would share my notions about Modernism. The notions of formulating futures and better societies, the need for an avant-garde, and the unquestioned authority of knowledge are all intertwined in an inextricable ideology that has the underlying assumption that good knowledge, good societies, and of course good architecture as well as good social science are *secular*. When we transmute, interpret and promote good architecture across a cultural divide with buildings, texts and images, they can become conflictive in most parts of the non-Western world, where the notion of *good* and *secular* do not coincide.

How then does one converse and interpret issues about what is good and not so good in non-secular societies? That is the bumpy road that I refer to, and it is on this that I search for critical companions.

There is a presumption in my text that the authority of knowledge is in considerable danger of being dismantled by real events. This presumption needs some explanation. Why else would there be a three-year project at the International Center for Advanced Studies at New York University called "The Authority of Knowledge in a Global Age?" Surely, when such a prestigious institution is worried about "the current sense of unease about the future that haunts the politics of the West and the daily lives of most people in the Global South", there is a need to stop and think. The problems of the potential dismantling of the authority of knowledge are clearly a serious business that is being attended to at the highest levels. Of course, this serious attention being given at such high levels worries me as a practising architect who has just begun to enjoy creating in the uncertainty of present times. I wonder how much time I will still have to wander about in the field of architecture offering solutions that range in scale from the micro to the macro. Some of these designed or creative solutions could be serious alternatives to the coercive solutions devised by military minds. For instance, I proposed in 2000 a shared railway line as a substitute for the concrete wall along the Palestine-Israel border. In this climate of uncertainty, when the irrefutable confidence in the social sciences has mercifully been suspended in disbelief, architects can work seriously in the fields of secular and non-secular domains, in the random and coincidental unfolding of events, in the geometric and geomantic logic of locations, in the chaotic and orderly expressions of forms, and (who knows) even within the parameters of science and para-science.

This then is my third expectation from critics. Consider not only the knowledge of the practitioner, but also his wisdom. There is a difference between knowledge and wisdom, and for many, if not most, parts of the Western world, the definitions and boundaries between knowledge and wisdom do not coincide. I am not using the word wisdom in a sense that defines the state of mind of an ageing recluse whose long hair is being blown about with the wind. By wisdom I mean the collective thought and convictions of a community that is not overshadowed by the gained knowledge of the Enlightenment. This wisdom seems to me to be a multi-dimensional amorphous body of thought capable of multiple interpretations, susceptible to last-minute consensus and influence, and not necessarily characterised by consistency of approach. It seems to me that the only permanent aspect of wisdom in architecture is probably the crucial role that negotiation plays in the interaction between the community and architecture.

I have talked about just three expectations that a practising architect has from critics (I have left out many more): celebrations of architecture, journeys across cultural divides, and expanding the expectations of architecture to become part of a wide range of activities in the field of architecture rather than being confined to a narrow street level view of architecture. The question now arises as to how such processes may be promoted in a world whose mediums are changing as fast as technology for representation and reproduction mutates from one form to another.

There are two aspects of promotion that seem to me to be vital in debating this issue. One is the rapidly declining attention span that audiences of architecture have when they scan it in the printed medium. The second is the growing centralisation of media ownership, which gives rise to all sorts of issues connected to the promotion of heroic architectural events and the important place of signature buildings that seem to capture longer attention spans. Both aspects are related to celebrating architecture at one level, but at the same time they are also totally disconnected from the real events that are beginning to change our lives in this century.

It would be easy to solve this dilemma if one knew where to look for solutions. Frankly, I cannot even begin to look for them. I just have a growing feeling that the new heroes of architecture will begin to emerge from outside the exclusive secular domain that has dominated architectural recognition so far. These heroes in all likelihood will be singled out by the kind of processes that institutions such as the Prince Claus Fund or the Aga Khan Award for Architecture carry out, and that are characterised by multiple interpretations of architecture, which end up as the only way to better understand this field.

On Culture and Architecture

MOUHSEN MAKSOUD

I would like to reflect on the relation between architecture and culture. In other words, how does our cultural perspective affect the way we view the architecture around us, whether we are architects, critics of architecture, or simply observers of it?

Foreign tourists would stand in front of a traditional Damascene house contemplating its entrance, which, although it does not exceed two metres in height, opens onto an unexpectedly wide space beyond. They wonder about the reason behind such a house design. Why does the traditional Damascene house appear to be a 'locked world' from the outside, while it is actually a welcoming 'open world' from the inside? Does this have to do with our traditional social values that emphasised segregation between women and men, and necessitated that women's living spaces be isolated from the outside world? Is this introverted house plan related to our need for privacy and secrecy, that is, our private world is our own and should not be revealed to others? Or is it intended to provide us with a sense of security against the outside world? I wonder whether Arab architects had a sort of Existentialist Sartrean disposition, believing in philosopher Jean-Paul Sartre's (d. 1980) maxim that "Hell is other people".

The amazement of the Western observer who tries to apprehend the features of the traditional Damascene house is not enough to inspire him to reproduce the same building style in his own world. The reason is that he, or she, belongs to a totally different culture.

In our Eastern world, however, we have a longing for this traditional architectural style, but we cannot replicate it anymore. This is because the Eastern architect, whether in Delhi or Damascus, lives the duality of the 'spiritual world' of the East and the 'progressive world' of the West. Although some Eastern architects have a longing for the embodiment of spirituality in their architecture, the inescapable effect of the overwhelmingly advanced West, especially in this age of globalisation, makes this very difficult to accomplish.

To what extent is architecture influenced both by the discourse on and the conflict of cultures? Have we reached a period where a new architectural style is emerging, a style we may call that of 'globalised architecture'?

Today, it is common to see Eastern cities that have a Western character. However, it is uncommon to see architecture with Eastern influences in the West. Our cities are losing their original character under the strong effects of Western culture. A change in cultural values is apparent in our societies and is being reflected on the architecture we produce. For example, our residences are no longer introverted, but extroverted. Interestingly enough, there is a resistance to this 'openness', which takes on various forms. Once a family moves into a house that has terraces overlooking the street, it starts introducing screens, whether of glass, cloth, or wood, to protect its privacy. Perhaps this attitude conveys a message to architects from the society they live in that it is acceptable to be inspired by others, but it is important that the end product be sensitive to our spiritual world. I think that we, as architects, are in desperate need to have a better understanding of the humanities.

If we architects lack the ability, time, and will to get involved in a quest for understanding the humanities, then maybe we are in need of architectural critics who have the necessary knowledge of these fields. The role of these critics is to widen our horizon and make us more aware of the problems we are creating but unable to perceive. Their role is to remind us that within the walls we build live human beings, each of whom has his or her spiritual needs. Moreover, in front of these walls pass people who are capable of judging our architecture as beautiful or ugly. Both beauty and ugliness are relative and subjective values that coexist, and their standards are developed according to our own cultural values.

Given that I come from an ancient world whose architecture goes back thousands of years, I would like to touch upon the relation between secular and sacred architecture. I believe that laicism had its effect on our architecture. The separation of religion from state is a political problem that is reflected in the separation of the place (the building) from the sacred. It is as if our world is still discoursing on architecture as it is still discoursing on politics.

I have so far expressed myself as an architect. Nevertheless, as the editor in chief of the Syrian magazine *Ibda'at Handasiyya* (Architectural Creations), I am aware of the crucial need for critics to inspire architects.

I believe there is a lack of journals specialised in architectural criticism. Moreover, schools of architecture, which already teach courses in the history of architecture, should start teaching courses in architectural criticism as part of their curricula. Maybe then we will become more aware of the intimate relation between architecture and the humanities.

III. CRITICISM AND THE MEDIA

The Power of Images

Manuel Cuadra

Unlike many architectural critics, I have no problem at all admiring the so-called 'star architects', who are not only 'stars', but also excellent architects. I also have no problem expressing my admiration for works by these star architects, which are not only spectacular, but also precious pieces of architecture. My interest is to study their works and try to understand what makes them so important for so many people. Since architecture today is communicated globally through photography and the media, including the Internet, I would like to link my subject to the role of photography and the media in architectural criticism.

We live in an increasingly complex world. Looking back at the twentieth century, particularly at twentieth-century architecture, it is clear that any attempt at reducing this complexity will fail quickly. In the early twentieth century, architects strongly believed – and many still do – in the necessity of social change as both a precondition for and a goal of architecture – more specifically, of a Modern architecture – that was adequate for the industrial age. Later on, we came to understand that true social progress is not as easy to achieve or define as we had hoped. The quality of the architecture of our cities in the twentieth century did not improve. On the contrary, quality was sacrificed in the name of a simple-minded functionalism, of a banally understood materialism, and, more precisely, of economic development.

As a reaction to this failure, we began to remember and to emphasise in our thinking the cultural dimension of architecture. We began to rediscover history and the importance of a well-understood historical continuity. We began to rediscover humanistic architectural theory, architecture as art, and the importance of providing a poetic dimension to all that we do as architects and urban planners, whether practitioners or theorists. Furthermore, as a reaction to other deficiencies of modern living, we have started to discover during the past few decades the ecological ramifications of our industrial era. We now understand that our survival at the global level requires seeing ourselves as part of nature, a nature that we have to learn to appreciate, take into account and respect in all our activities.

How may we create an architecture that allows us to address the dramatic situation and the global scale of the social, ecological and cultural challenges we face today? Surprisingly, at least a few leading architects over the past few decades have refused to be paralysed by this situation. They have been motivated to explore different paths than those stipulated by the Modern Movement at its beginnings. They have abandoned the idea of an absolute, permanently objective architecture, and instead have let their instincts guide them. All over the world, not only are we witnessing the emergence of iconic buildings – buildings of an extremely powerful formal appearance – we are also observing an unexpectedly euphoric public resonance to these works of architecture. When was the last time that people felt inspired by architecture in such a way and at such a global scale?

To include 'instinct' as a guiding force in the design process of creating forms and their meanings constitutes by itself a challenge for architectural theory and criticism. In view of the complexities of today's world, even the most elaborate works of architecture are unable to provide anything more than simple answers to highly multifaceted situations. By adding a subjective dimension such as that of instinct, it becomes even harder to understand, explain or judge what architects are doing. Under such circumstances, architectural criticism becomes more necessary than ever to help explain what architects are doing. In a certain way, architectural critics assume the role of a conscience; they can help architects as well as the public to better understand the needs of our cities and urban communities, and what architecture is (or is not) achieving for them. However, when dealing with 'iconic' buildings, architectural criticism will have to reach its full potential in order to reach the level of relevance that such buildings ask for and deserve.

As critics, our main instrument is discourse, that is, the word. However, we also work with images, which form a part of our lectures and writings. Images constitute a fundamental link between what architects do and the public, which in many cases perceives works of architecture through the media only. In spite of the difficulties involved in reducing architectural forms and spaces to the two dimensional composition of an image, images nonetheless transmit a great deal. They contain and condense much information that is embedded in architectural forms and spaces, information of a basically cultural – and often subconscious – nature that is expressed through the non-verbal language of architecture. That information naturally resides in a realm that is beyond the objective aspects of the building, beyond its function and method of construction, and so on. To speak about the power of images in architecture is to make reference to the subjective side of architecture, which is about the many associations, intuitions and sensations that architecture evokes and causes in the spectator.

The amount of information that may be condensed and embedded in architectural images is expressed clearly in figure 1. It is an image that is widely recognised worldwide: the Acropolis or upper city of Athens. In fact, this is one of the strongest architectural images to have come out of Western European civilisation. In it, we see many things. We see fragments of a natural landscape that initially was transformed into a cultural landscape, accommodating agricultural production. We do

Fig. 1. The Acropolis or upper city of Athens.

not see much of the city, but we see the site of the old fortress. We see the massive rock that constitutes the base on which the fortress rested.

This fortress was the place from which a whole area was ruled. It was the source of order, and simultaneously a source of violence and oppression for the people of the area. As the image informs us through the superposition of the fortress next to the Parthenon, at a certain moment in history, however, the function of the Acropolis dramatically changed. The dictators and their fortress were wiped out. Since then, the Acropolis has housed on its top the house of the gods as the new personification of what unifies the population of Athens; no longer was it violence, but a common faith and common convictions. It is relevant for our subject of inquiry that this profound political, social and cultural transformation, with all its complexity, is contained in one single image, that of the Acropolis. We may deduce that if this image is so important to us, then this definitely is not primarily because of its aesthetic qualities, but because of the human relevance of the story it implies and permanently tells.

Immobilien

Das Wunder von Bilbao

Majestätisch thront das berühmte Guggenheim-Museum am Flußufer. Das Gebäude hat der Stadt nicht nur ein neues Image, sondern auch viel Geld und manchen Arbeitsplatz eingebracht.

Das Baskenland setzt Spitzenarchitektur als Werbung ein. Touristen kommen in Scharen. Im Weinanbaugebiet Rioja baut Frank O. Gehry.

Fig. 2. Frank Gehry's Guggenheim Museum in Bilbao (1997) featured in "Das Wunder von Bilbao", *Frankfurter Allgemeine Zeitung* (*FAZ*; 16.10. 2005).

The Acropolis of course is an exceptional case, but not a unique one. Frank Gehry's Guggenheim Museum in Bilbao (1997) demonstrates a building criticised by many architectural critics, because of its use – or misuse, as they would say – of aesthetically powerful images merely to achieve spectacular effects that attract media attention. I would like to present an image of it that was published in a newspaper as part of an article entitled "Das Wunder von Bilbao" (The Wonder of Bilbao). This article does not have much to do with architecture, but deals with the 'Bilbao effect': the positive consequences of spectacular architecture for a city. The article praises the transformations Bilbao has undergone and the international reputation it has gained as a result of a single work of architecture. The article was published in *Frankfurter Allgemeine Zeitung* (*FAZ*; 16 October 2005), Germany's primary newspaper. However, instead of being featured in the newspaper's cultural section, which is where one would normally expect an article dealing with such a building to appear, the article appeared in the newspaper's real estate section. It is an impressive achievement for good architecture to enter the realm of real estate reporting, generally dedicated exclusively to commercial buildings. Moreover, the article has little to do with architectural criticism. It is purely a work of journalism. In this context, it is typical in journalistic articles to reduce a number of potential im-

78

ages that may be included in the article to only one; although the image presented in this article on Bilbao is a strong one, it does not satisfy expectations from the perspective of architectural criticism (fig. 2). Not only is that one image not enough, but it also gives a wrong impression of how the visitor actually experiences the building.

In fact, once in Bilbao, the spectator is confronted with an extremely complex set of images (figs. 3–8). Of course, there is the so-called 'metal flower', the main composition topping the complex, and for which it is mainly known. However, as one walks along the river promenade from the city centre towards the museum, it is not the 'metal flower' that initially meets us in the foreground, but a strange stone tower and an enormous highway bridge. None of these elements appears in the photograph accompanying the newspaper article. As one continues walking, the museum suddenly disappears below the bridge. Following that, the long, plastic-shaped stone body located underneath the bridge, and connecting the stone tower to the main building with the 'metal flower', can be perceived. From the bridge, the impressions of the museum are very different. As one further approaches the museum, the stone tower turns out to be not a massive structure, but a light steel skeleton with a very thin layer of stone sheathing. This is only one of a number of unexpected details that step by step give new dimensions to this piece of architecture. Besides the many mysteriously shaped, but nonetheless highly photogenic sculptural elements that continuously jump into the scene, there are the more basic architectural decisions that reveal the inner structure of the museum and its way of dealing with the surroundings. There is, for example, the distinction between the parts of the facades covered in sheet metal and those covered in stone. One may ask why that is. In the same way, other details confront us in many other situations that we cannot spontaneously understand through rational means.

There are interesting parallels between Bilbao and the Acropolis affecting both form and content. The formal similarities may appear to be more apparent: the remaining ruins of the stone base of the fortress in Athens seem to correspond to the lower parts of the museum. The Parthenon is a 'light' structure that emerges from the rock, not unlike the 'metal flower' topping the Guggenheim complex. The more interesting question is whether there are parallels in the cultural content behind these forms; that is, between the historical drama we know about the Acropolis and whatever happened in Bilbao. There are such parallels, at least if we are willing to follow the stories told to us by the images.

In view of the way that industry beginning in the nineteenth century had consumed the originally idyllic landscape of the area surrounding the small-scale medieval city of Bilbao, it is difficult to imagine how beautiful Bilbao and its surroundings had been until then. The images of the industrial area extending from the port to the old city persisted until only a few years ago; they expressed not only a high degree of visual contamination of the landscape and corrosion of the image of the

3.

4.

5.

6.

7.

8.

Fig. 3. As one walks along the river promenade from
the centre of Bilbao towards the Guggenheim Museum,
it is not the 'metal flower' that initially meets us in the foreground,
but a strange stone tower and an enormous highway bridge.

Fig. 4. As one continues walking along the river promenade
from the centre of Bilbao towards the Guggenheim Museum,
the building suddenly disappears below the bridge.

Figs. 5–7. As one approaches the Guggenheim Museum,
its stone tower turns out to be not a massive structure,
but a light steel skeleton with a very thin layer of stone sheathing.

Fig. 8. General view of the Guggenheim Museum.

Fig. 9. The site before construction began on the Guggenheim Museum in the 1990s.

city, but also severe pollution of the soil, air and river. This is a one-sided view of the advent of heavy industry to the city. The other side of the story is the wealth that industry generated for Bilbao. To release the city from this ambivalent dependence on heavy industry was not only possible, but also vitally necessary for Bilbao when its industrial base collapsed as a consequence of economic tertiarisation and globalisation during the late twentieth century. Figure 9 shows the site as it existed before construction began on the Guggenheim Museum in the 1990s, with large ships entering the river to reach the heart of the city. The visual blight characterising the area is evident in this image.

All of this is relevant here because Frank Gehry had a decisive influence on the choice of the site of the museum. In fact, the city of Bilbao originally had offered the Guggenheim Foundation to locate the museum on a prominent site in the city, but Gehry rejected this offer and instead proposed to go with what he conceived as the new heart of Bilbao, not the cultural centre, but where the city had most deteriorated. He undoubtedly had practical reasons for his decision, such as the strategic location of the site and its untouched potential. The prominence given to the site in Athens by the rock is given to the site in Bilbao by its particular position in a valley along the river. However, Gehry must also have been aware of the transformation that this area had to undergo: a transformation as dramatic and transcendental as the one that took place in Athens when the first temple – a predecessor of the Parthenon – was built on top of the old fortress.

With this idea in mind, Gehry's proposal may be understood for what it is: the proposal was not one of an isolated object – as spectacular as such an arrangement might be – as suggested by photographic images including the one used by *FAZ*. Gehry initiated a transformation process that finally led to an intricate new order for the city and to the crystallisation of a new spirit of the place. An expression of this at a smaller scale is the poetic dialogue that the museum has developed with its surroundings as a whole, and particularly with the large-scale elements that remain from the city's industrial past.

The goal of this interpretation is to make clear that the stories behind a work of architecture that deserves this qualification cannot be experienced without exposing oneself to it as well as to its place, details, atmosphere and magic. The spirit of the site and of a building can hardly be transmitted by 480 x 640-pixel images through the Internet. Consequently, there cannot be an architectural criticism that deserves this qualification based on such images. Still, even a whole set of images may not prove to be sufficient. What we really need is a combination of criticism and photography: an intelligent and critical approach, not just documentary photography that merely reflects the complexity of the city and of architecture – for good and for bad.

Seen this way, the problem of 'media architecture' is not a problem of architecture, but of the media. The problem specifically takes place when the media reduces architecture to what it considers to be communicable or of public interest without seriously taking into account what is necessary for understanding architecture.

The Role of the Media and Photography in Architectural Criticism

DOĞAN HASOL

True architectural criticism is based on examining the real building in question and considering the views of its creators and users. However, this is not always possible, and therefore evaluations and criticisms are often made on the basis of photographs and printed publications.

Years ago, criticism was to be found primarily in the local media, particularly in regional publications and periodicals. Before that, only international activities such as large-scale exhibitions and publications with cross-national readerships provided information on architectural products like the Crystal Palace (1851), the Eiffel Tower (1889) and the Barcelona Pavilion (1928–1929).

In those days, architects and critics from countries with international languages were particularly fortunate. Publications in languages such as English, French, or German were read over a wide geographical area and by a great number of readers. This advantage enjoyed by an international language is still valid today for English, and publications in English still enjoy a marked advantage in the breadth of their appeal. Indeed, in order to reach a wider readership, publications in many countries employ English alongside their native languages. English has become the modern "Esperanto".

The ease of communication in the electronic environment that the rapid development of digital photographic technologies provides today has been of great advantage to architecture critics and publicists, as well as to readers. Thanks to the combination of digital photography and the Internet, photographs can now be sent to almost every corner of the world without any limitation in time or space. The possibility of showing these photographs on the Internet has opened up new horizons for all. This new development has removed, to a certain extent, the differences between large and small countries.

Architectural exhibitions can be launched on the Internet. It is now possible to arrange exhibitions that can be viewed twenty-four hours a day from anywhere in the world (www.archmuseum.org for example). Besides, the Internet now makes it possible to easily arrange design competitions on an international scale. We witnessed very successful applications of this facility during the International Union of Architects (UIA) 2005 Istanbul World Congress of Architecture. Architectural critics can also exploit recent developments in photography and information technology. Thanks to the large number of photographs and the extensive information now available, they can base their criticism on a much more reliable foundation.

Film and television have also widened the scope for critics of architecture. Years ago, a number of films that had no direct connection with architecture resulted in transforming architecture into a desirable profession. In a number of these films, the main character was an architect. Post-war American films (more particularly after the 1950s) treating architectural subjects were found inspiring in many parts of the world and were followed by several films directly devoted to architectural topics. Naturally, there were always documentaries on architecture, which thanks to television are presently being shown in various parts of the world and are arousing interest in several countries. The *Design 360* programme is one interesting example. Because of these films and documentaries, design and architecture have become popular professions with the younger generation. At the same time, they have provided critics with new means for expressing their thoughts and opinions.

Will the Internet replace printed publications? This is a very controversial topic. I believe that each will retain its own individual place.

We also need to consider the effects of animated images on the Internet. At present, architectural images on the Internet are often in the form of still photographs, but this is changing as an increasing number of such images is being animated. This will allow a much better depiction of architectural works and their interiors.

Where does architectural criticism stand in the face of all these developments in information technology? Criticism of architecture still appears mainly in books, periodicals and a few documentaries. It seems to me that critics are not making full and effective use of Internet facilities. Although there has been a great development in architectural publications on the Internet, architectural criticism using this medium has not yet attained the level and quantity it has reached in printed publications. Nevertheless, the web offers completely new possibilities for the examination and discussion of architectural topics, and has become a field in which young people who are taking their first steps in the architectural profession can engage in lively discussion. However, these discussions are still far from displaying the quality of truly professional architectural criticism, and professional architecture critics still play very little part in them. This leads us to ask whether the average age of critics of architecture determines their ability to adjust to current developments in the Internet.

The website referenced in this essay was accessed in May 2006.

The Nature of Architectural Criticism

HANI RASHID

I practise and teach architecture in various places, and it strikes me as interesting how criticism and journalism focused on architecture differ so substantially from culture to culture, era to era, and audience to audience. Despite the onslaught of what author and public policy advocate Jeremy Rifkin calls the "generation @", a condition of hyper-mobility and electronically tethered cultures, and of people no longer connected by geographic conditions but by information streams and economic vectors that traverse the globe, there prevails an uncanny condition of a fluid, seamless state of existence that is obviously impacting people, cities and architecture. Criticism, and sometimes mere commentary, seems at times rather narrowly focused on issues that are more local in scope and scale, often failing to engage some of the larger forces of influence that impact architects and urbanists around the globe. So why is this the case? Are we still in a hangover situation in regard to Modernism and the International Style, thinking that their inflated promises, so rampant in the mid to late twentieth century, had resulted only in failure, especially with respect to locality and difference? Perhaps there is a deeper sense of purpose on the part of critics to temper attitudes against subjects seemingly more stable and accessible to their audiences. All this raises the question of who is actually the audience for architectural criticism?

It is impossible to generalise about architectural criticism and journalism, given the diversity of sources for published criticism. The popular press, including highly-respected, 'serious' newspapers such as *El País*, *The Guardian*, or *The New York Times*, which, for better or worse, constitute some of the most ubiquitous and widely read sources of information, obviously speak to audiences at large. They need to maintain a global perspective, while juggling local concerns, politics and tastes. Yet, we then find ourselves caught in a dilemma where critical issues are more often than not seen through a Madrid, London, or New York point of view. Then, of course, there are the various journals, ranging from the academic to those destined for the trade, such as *Architecture* in the United States, France's *L'Architecture d'Aujourd'hui*, Iran's *Memar*, the METU *Journal of the Faculty of Architecture* from Turkey, *A+U* from Japan, and *Space* from South Korea, all of which speak more specifically to architects, and perhaps – though not as much as they should – to builders, clients and other design professionals. These publications often attempt to "set the bar", so to speak, to give recognition and endorsement to architects and works that have been judged to be of significance and to have achieved a high enough standard. Here, we find voices that struggle with global and local issues in both the qualitative and technical aspects of architecture. In many ways, these journals, the best of them at least, struggle to incorporate academic interests and debate on a more philosophical footing, whenever possible, often engaging both global and local issues. In addition to these two forms of dissemination, there are the somewhat problematic, yet necessary and influential, popular publications such as *Wallpaper*, *Icon* and *Casa Brutus* that cater only to global audiences with a form of criticism that, albeit superficial, supports an insatiable appetite for identifying stylistic trends and discovering the ever-changing and ineffable notion of the 'new'. In sharp contrast to these ubiquitous magazines and Internet publications, we have the unfortunately almost extinct breed of academic journals, which, like their counterparts in other disciplines, are focused on the fielding of ideas and criticism to a rarefied and specialised audience. Because of this, they often render their content inaccessible, and therefore of little interest to those outside their targeted audience. Most notably, in the United States we had *Oppositions* in the 1970s, *Assemblage* in the 1980s, *ANY* in the 1990s, and a small handful of journals today such as *Log* and *Volume* (the latter being a collaboration between the Office of Metropolitan Architecture, the Dutch journal *Archis* and Columbia University's CLAB). And last but by no means least is the Internet and the advent of the blogsphere, a veritable tidal wave in the world of architectural criticism, with an impact not yet profoundly felt but certain to be of influence in the not-too-distant future.

All this raises a series of questions: what is the role of criticism in architecture today? How is it changing, and who are its audiences? What are the motives and intentions behind forming sound criticism? What is the role of today's populist journals? Will academic journals survive and regain their relevance? Also, what about the blogsphere? Is it forging a pathway where criticism will assume a relevant, compelling global and local voice of worth and impact, or is it proving to be too unfiltered and uncontrollable to be a place from which real criticism emerges and in which it thrives?

IV. KUWAIT CITY THROUGH THE EYES OF AN ARCHITECTURAL PHOTOGRAPHER

PHOTOS BY KAMRAN ADLE
TAKEN IN DECEMBER 2005

1. Kuwait City on a foggy morning in December 2005.

2.

3.

4.

5.

6.

2. Kuwait Water Towers, VBB Consulting
Engineers and Björn & Björn Design, 1976.

3, 4, 6. The Red Palace, al-Jahra Town, 1914–1915.

5. Ruins of Bayt al-Ghanem (Sheikh Khaz'al's house)
in Kuwait City, early 20th century.

7–10. The coexistence of traditional nomadic
and contemporary lifestyles characterises Kuwait today.

Following pages
11. Fishing dhows in the busy harbour, waterside mosques
and the bustling business district of Kuwait City.

7.

8.

9.

12.

13.

12, 13. The vibrant souks of Kuwait City.

14. Souk al-Hout (fish market),
al-Sharq Waterfront, Kuwait City, KEO
International Consultants, 1998.

15. Souk al-Zal in the restored old
Central Business District, Kuwait City,
Pan Arab Consulting Engineers, 1999.

14.

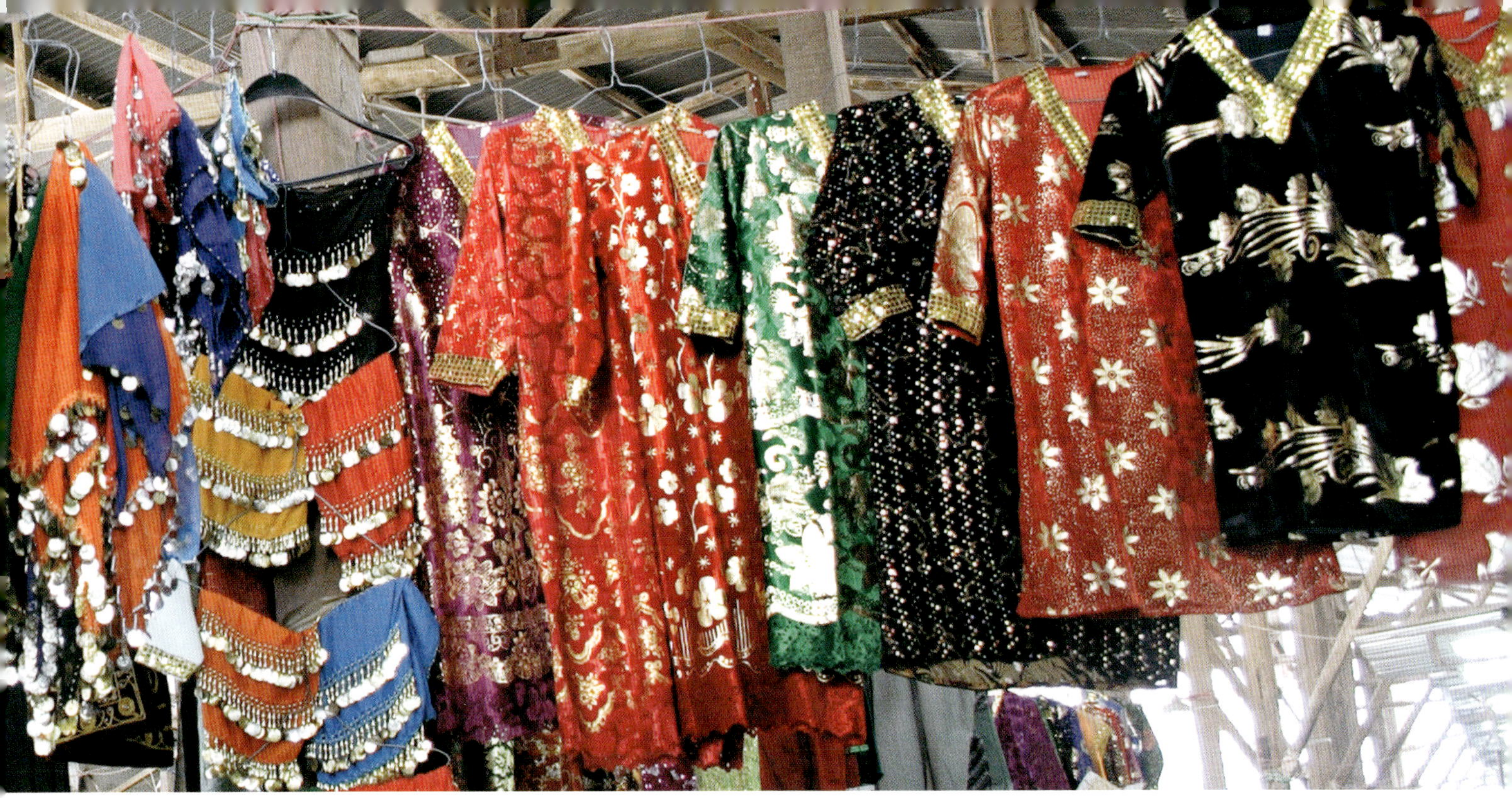

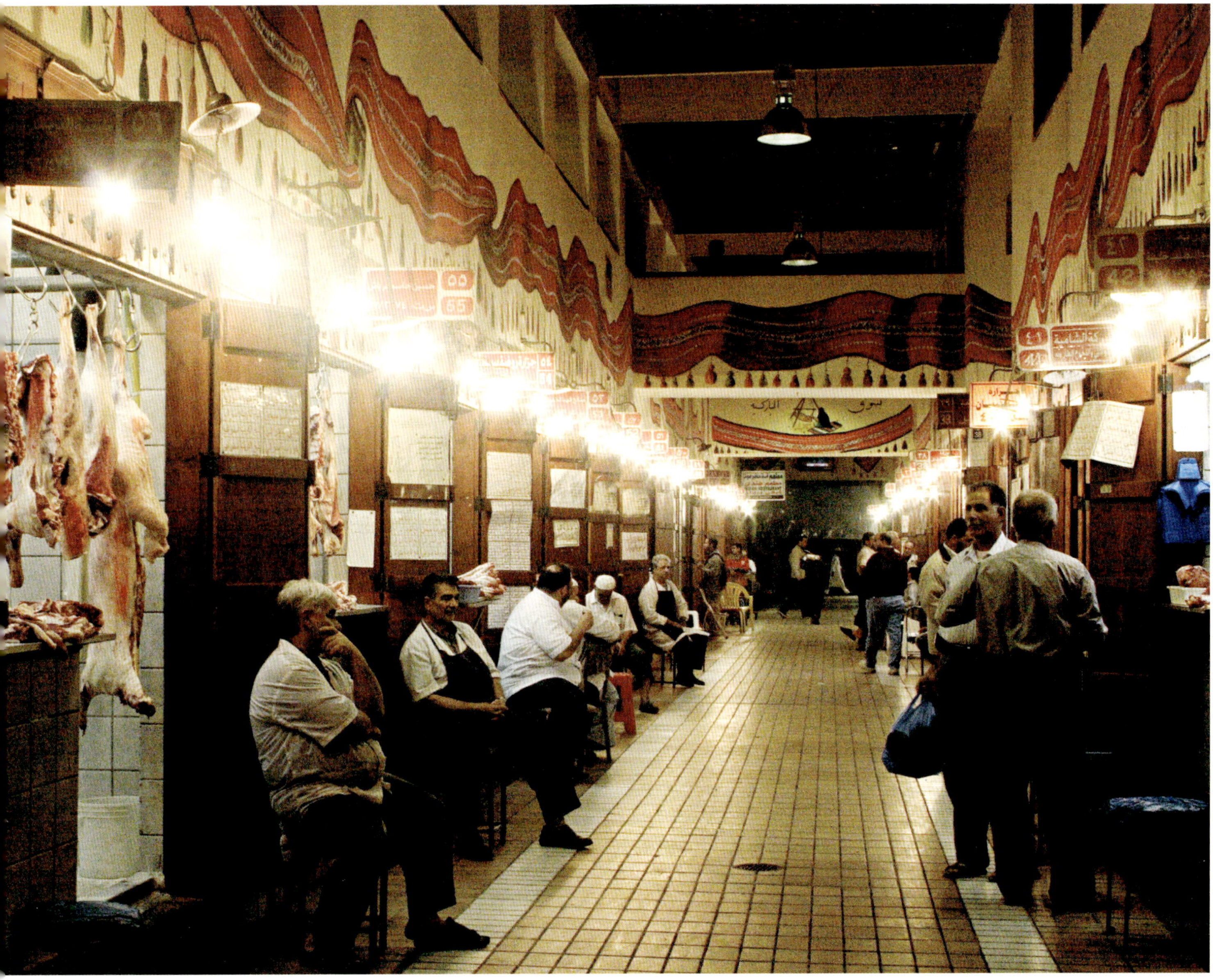

5.

16.

17.

18.

19. Minaret of an old mosque overshadowed by a more recent office building, Kuwait City.

20. Gold Souk, Kuwait City, Pan Arab Consulting Engineers, 1982.

16. Residential Complex, al-Salimiyya, late 1960s.

17. A public school destroyed during the Iraqi invasion of Kuwait has been kept as a reminder of the 1990 war.

18. A concrete facade with ground floor arcades is typical of the architecture of Kuwait City during the 1970s.

19.

21, 22. Kuwait National Museum, Kuwait City,
Michel Ecochard, 1977.

23. Kuwait Towers, Kuwait City, VBB Consulting
Engineers and Björn & Björn Design, 1976.

24. An office and residential quarter
in Kuwait City today.

25. Residential complex, Public Authority
for Housing Welfare, Kuwait City.

26. Ahmad al-Jaber Street, Kuwait City.

Following pages
27. Main prayer hall, Great Mosque, Kuwait City,
Makiya Associates, 1986.

21.

22.

23.

24.

25.

26.

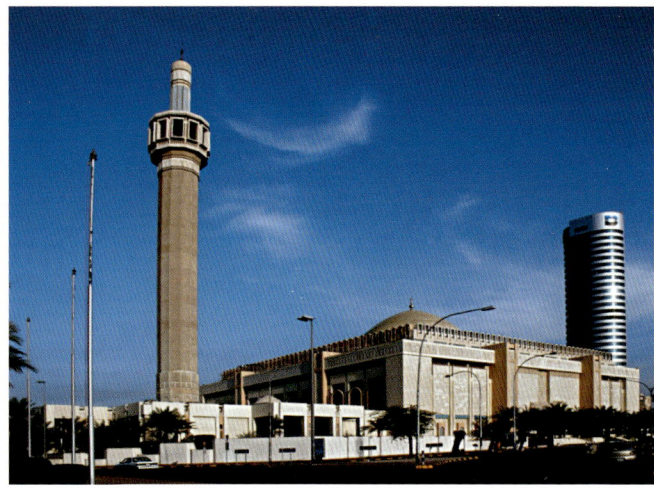

28.

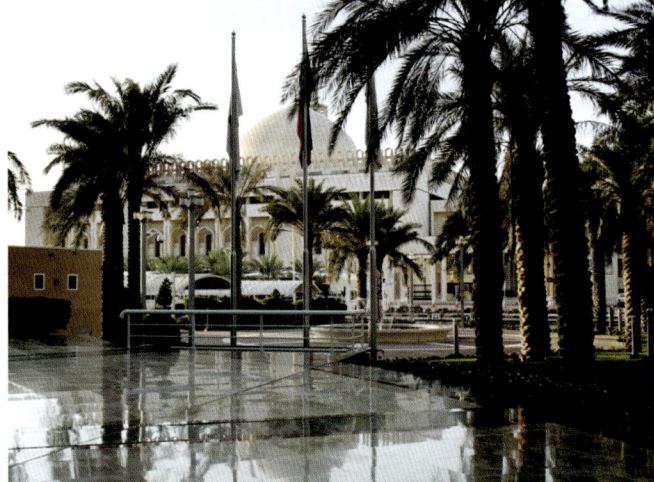

29.

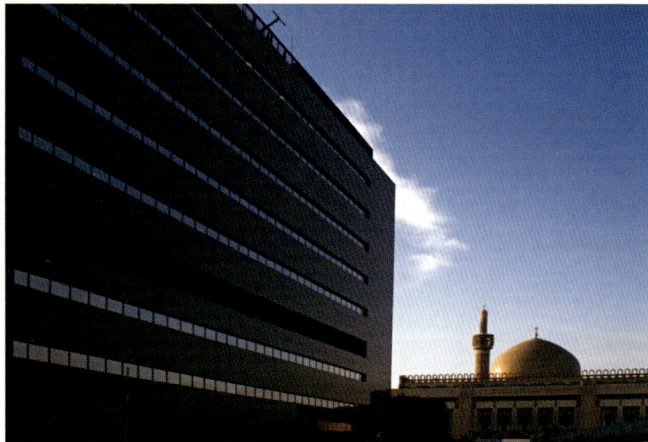

30.

28–31. Great Mosque, Kuwait City,
Makiya Associates, 1986.

31.

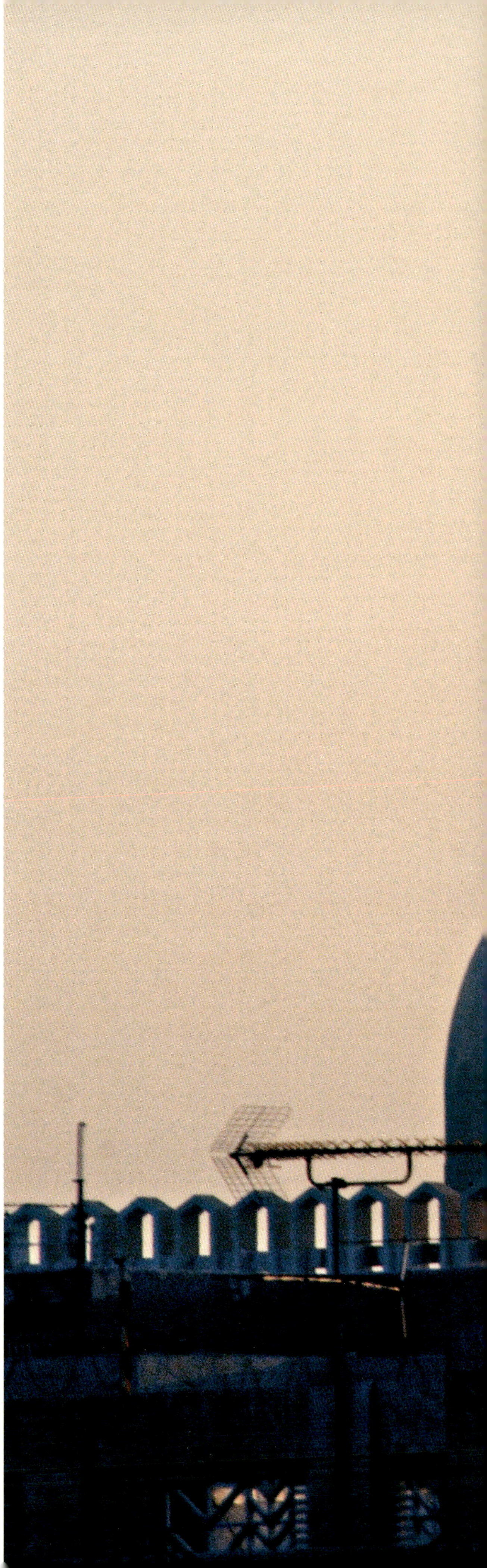

32.

33.

34.

37.

32–34. Liberation Tower, Kuwait City,
Electrowatt Engineering Services, 1996.

35, 36. Al-Sharq residential/commercial area, Kuwait City.

37. Al-Shahid Tower, al-Sharq, Kuwait City.

Following pages
38. Al-Sharq Waterfront, Kuwait City,
KEO International Consultants, 1998.

39.

40.

42.

39, 40, 42. Al-Sharq Waterfront, Kuwait City, KEO International Consultants, 1998.

41. Kuwait Port Authority, Shuwaikh, 1992.

43. Kuwait University, Kuwait City, Pan Arab Consulting Engineers, 2000.

41.

44.

45.

47.

44. Courtyard of the Great Mosque,
Kuwait City, Makiya Associates, 1986.

45. Kuwait Stock Exchange, Kuwait City,
John S. Bonnington Partnership, 1984.

46. Al-Awadi Towers, Ahmad al-Jaber Street,
Kuwait City.

47. Residential Complex, Kuwait City,
Saleh al-Mutawwa', 1995.

48. Chamber of Commerce and Industry,
Kuwait City, HLW International LLP
and Al-Jazeera Consultants, 1999.

49. Ahmad al-Jaber Street, Kuwait City.

46.

50.

51.

52.

50. Dasman Specialised Diabetes Treatment
and Research Centre, Kuwait City, Gulf Consultant
and Cambridge Seven Associates, 2004.

51, 52. Kuwait University, Kuwait City,
Pan Arab Consulting Engineers, 2000.

53. A building boom that has taken place after 2000
characterises the al-Sharq area in Kuwait City.

54.

54. Arraya Shopping Centre and the
Courtyard Hotel, Kuwait City,
Pan Arab Consulting Engineers, 2003.

55. Residential building, Kuwait City.

57.

58.

59.

56. Holiday Inn Hotel, Kuwait City, 2006.

57, 58. Al-Sharq Waterfront, Kuwait City,
KEO International Consultants, 1998.

59. Madinat al-Fahaheel, Kuwait City,
Dar Al-Omran/Rasem Badran with
Gulf Consultants, Pan Arab Consulting
Engineers, Option One, and OHA
Engineering Consultants, 2004.

60.

60. A busy street in Kuwait City, which
is striving to re-establish its prominence
as an urban centre in the booming Gulf region.

V. ARCHITECTURAL PUBLISHING
AND JOURNALISM IN THE ISLAMIC WORLD

The Impact of Architectural Criticism
on Iranian Architecture after the Islamic Revolution

KAMRAN AFSHAR NADERI

The Islamic Revolution of 1978 had a deep impact on Iranian intellectuals and artists. The consciousness of being in a new period and having the historical opportunity to develop innovative ideas, far from Western paradigms, persuaded the intellectuals of the country to explore new directions that were often characterised by spontaneity. In this, architecture was no exception. To think differently about architecture started at the universities. After unsuccessful attempts by politically motivated students to review the programmes of university faculties, the government closed down all universities in the country for two years under the pretext of carrying out a cultural revolution. In 1983, the universities were reopened with completely new, but inadequate and extempore, programmes. The discipline of architecture entered into an uncertain state. The authorities declared architecture an extravagance that was unnecessary for society. In fact, most students who studied architecture abroad did not receive any scholarships from the government. Moreover, they were not even permitted to receive allowances from their families. Architecture was treated as an anti-revolutionary profession.

In order to overcome this crisis affecting architecture, architects searched for new expressions and a new identity that ideologically would justify their work. Simplistic readings of architecture consequently emerged. This was evident especially in how the adjective "Islamic" was only attributed to the historical architecture of the Islamic period, and achieving architectural forms worthy of being called Islamic was expressed through an obsession with creating forms that revealed a visible and superficial relationship to the past.

During the 1980s, no important contributions to architecture were made in Iran. A predominant intolerance in society did not allow space for architectural criticism. Quantity prevailed over quality; poverty was appreciated as part of a new value system; and beauty was looked down upon as a symbol of aristocratic privilege. These were natural consequences of the Revolution, and all had negative effects on the field of architecture.

The period following the Iran-Iraq war, which ended in 1988, modified most of these developments. A new appreciation of art and architecture emerged among Iranians. The authorities also realised that architecture could be used as an efficient instrument for propaganda, and they consequently supported efforts that could help develop an official architectural style for the Islamic Republic.

At the beginning of the 1990s, the Ministry of Housing and Urban Development established *Abadi*, one of the first important architectural magazines to emerge following the Iranian Revolution. It also launched a number of cultural activities, including conferences, seminars, exhibitions and competitions that often indirectly led to unexpected and contradictory results that were not necessarily in line with official policies.

A most important architectural event of the post-revolutionary period was a competition in 1994 to build a complex for the Iran Academies in the centre of Tehran. The building site is situated in a large and vacant area that was designated during the Shah's period as the Capital's administrative and cultural core. The competition jury selected a project by architect S. Hadi Mirmiran. However, the authorities rejected this selection, because of some references it made to pre-Islamic architectural traditions in Iran, and considered it too bold and irreverent. Instead, a rather irrelevant project that incorporated the usual necessary eclectic elements borrowed from Islamic architectural traditions was chosen. The main problem with Mirmiran's project paradoxically was that its remarkable and unexpected beauty could still irritate the authorities. In order to avoid such an embarrassing situation in future competitions, the jury members for the next public competition were chosen carefully to conform to officially sanctioned formal and aesthetic tastes. Mirmiran's project, outstanding among the other entries for its simplicity and strong form, was the first brilliant example of a historicist trend in architectural design that appeared during the post-revolutionary period. In 1994, I wrote an article evaluating this project, and the article most likely was the first work of architectural criticism to appear in the post-revolution period.[1]

By the second half of the 1990s, Iran witnessed a number of events that had a deep impact on the country's architecture. One of these events was the creation of the architecture department at the Islamic Azad University, the first university to be established in Iran without governmental financial support, which also meant that governmental control over the university was relatively limited. The university also had branches throughout the country. Another development was the election of the reformist Mohammad Khatami in 1997 as president, which brought more freedoms to intellectuals and journalists. This period also witnessed the launching of hundreds of new periodicals, at least a dozen of which were devoted to architecture. In addition, the increase in oil prices on the international level resulted in achieving higher living standards for Iranians. Travel restrictions were also eased, as well as restrictions on importing Western books and magazines. Finally, this period witnessed the spread of satellite dishes and the Internet.

As a consequence of these various developments, the obsession with the issues of national identity and history was suddenly abandoned. There was a renewed interest in becoming part of the international community and keeping up with the "spirit of the time". In architecture, these new sentiments were expressed in the phenomenon of Iranian architects copying some of the most visually expressive examples of radical trends in Western architecture. Architects including Rem Koolhaas, Peter Eisenman, Frank Gehry and Greg Lynn were treated as idols. Students, supported mostly by younger teachers, proposed bold projects that were inspired by the works of these international architects. Although the work of students seemed to be in line with vanguard trends, there was a deep lack of original ideas in their projects, which were highly derivative in nature.

Memar magazine, founded in 1997, was a turning point in the evolution of architectural culture in Iran. The goal of this magazine has mainly been to discover and highlight talents and original ideas among Iranian architects residing inside and outside the country.

Architectural criticism also benefited from the new and dynamic atmosphere created by the newly emerging young generation of architects. By the beginning of the new millennium, the number of professionals dedicated to architectural criticism had significantly increased. One could come across many works worthy of evaluation by critics in comparison with the previous decade. In fact a number of young architects achieved fame during this period largely because of the writings that addressed their designs.

During the last few years, the Iranian Architects Society has organised a number of events, including conferences, seminars, exhibitions and competitions. Exhibitions have usually been coupled with presentations that provide an opportunity for discussing the exhibited works. In 2001, *Memar* magazine launched the first award in Iran for completed projects. The jury deliberations for the award were published fully in the magazine.

During recent years, architectural criticism has offered considerable support to progressive architects who are not part of the establishment, and has helped establish their confidence regarding their potential and talent. Architectural critics, aware of two extreme threats – imitating international star architects on the one hand, and designing pastiche works based on historical models on the other –, encouraged independent trends among architects.

The 2004 *Memar* award for architecture illustrates this development. Among the numerous entries submitted for the award that year, those by architects of the previous generation and architects affiliated with the political establishment were eliminated early on in the jury deliberations. There were also two women among the winners. All the winning projects had their roots in a consciousness of real conditions and of limitations governing the process of architectural creation in Iran. The projects concentrated on the treatment of space, and none of them attempted to create forced striking visual effects.

As the latest cycle of the *Memar* award was announced in 2005, it has become obvious that the new generation of architects in Iran is no longer interested in simply following the latest architectural trends, but is undertaking independent paths based on a deep study of local issues and on personal creativity.

At present, there are tens of professionals in Iran involved in architectural criticism. The quality of the articles and publications has reached internationally acceptable standards. There are still serious shortcomings, such as the lack of specialised university programmes in architectural criticism, the lack of a professional association for architectural critics, and a shortage of events related to architectural criticism. The achievements made, nonetheless, have been remarkable.

[1] See Kamran Afshar Naderi, "A Criticism on Theoretical Fundamentals of Iran's Academies Project", in *Architecture et Urbanisme*, 28–29, 1994, pp. 30–36.

Architectural Publications in Egypt

MOHAMED A. IBRAHIM

Architecture in Egypt during the twentieth century may be divided into two phases: the first being from 1900 to 1950, and the second from 1950 to 2000. During the first phase, architectural production flourished, and a considerable number of important buildings were constructed with the participation of internationally renowned architects. The works of architecture of the period included public buildings, as well as royal and residential complexes, all of which expressed high standards of artistic production. This was accompanied by considerable cultural growth and an impressive level of aesthetic sense. The public also expressed its views on architecture, and helped define the nature and character of architecture.

During the second phase, such developments slowed down, primarily due to Egypt's involvement in the Arab-Israeli conflict. After Egypt's victory in the 1973 war, there was a huge reconstruction and development movement in the country. Numerous distinguished projects were completed, and many architectural competitions and conferences were organised. Unfortunately, we suffer from a lack of documentation and a lack of publications relating to the buildings developed during this period. Besides, until recently, this architectural revival was not accompanied by an upgrading of our schools of architecture or a reassessment of their curricula. In addition, the role of the Egyptian Engineers Syndicate in developing architectural culture has been non-existent, and that of the Architectural Society has been very limited. Moreover, today there are no Egyptian periodicals dedicated to architecture. Consequently, there is a great need for a strong and influential organisation that would protect the interest of architects, upgrade their knowledge and unify their efforts.

Concerning the history of architectural publications in Egypt during the modern period, the first architectural journal, *Alemara* (*al-'Imara*; Architecture), was established in 1939 by architect Sayyid Kurayyim. This periodical, of which up to ten issues appeared every year, ceased publication from 1943 to 1945 during World War II, but resumed publication after the war until 1959, when it was closed down because of conflicts between Sayyid Kurayyim and Egyptian president Jamal 'Abd al-Nasir. The total number of issues of *Alemara* that appeared during this twenty-year period was sixty-seven.

In 1945, the Egyptian Engineers Syndicate launched its own periodical, *Majallat al-Muhandisin* (The Engineers' Magazine), which continues to appear up to this day. It addresses the various fields of engineering, including architecture, but only provides architectural subjects with very limited coverage. In 1980, the Architectural Society published its own biannual publication, entitled *al-Majalla al-Mi'mariyya* (The Architectural Magazine), but it only appeared for ten years. Following that came an art and architecture magazine entitled *Madina*, which was sponsored by architects Tamer Zakaria, Ali Gabr and Amr Abdel Kawi. This monthly magazine appeared from 1998 until 2001. A total of twenty-one issues of *Madina* was published.

Alam Al Bena (The World of Construction) magazine was established in 1980 by my late father Abdel Baki Ibrahim and his late partner Hazem Ibrahim through the Centre for Planning and Architectural Studies (CPAS). 216 issues of this magazine were published until 1999, when it ceased publication because of lack of funding. *Alam Al Bena* was an Arabic-language publication that also featured a few English-language sections. It was well known to architects and students of architecture in Egypt and the Arab world. It presented a wide spectrum of international works as well as important local projects and architectural competitions. It also reviewed various theoretical, technical and critical subjects. Moreover, it offered opportunities for architectural criticism. The purpose behind the magazine was to revive our local culture and Islamic heritage, and to encourage the adaptation of modern technologies that are appropriate to our climate, resources, and living conditions, as well as to the needs of the local community. It had a great impact on increasing architectural awareness amongst several generations of architects.

In addition to publishing *Alam Al Bena*, CPAS organised monthly cultural evenings for architects that included screening films on architecture, interviewing important architects, and discussing issues of importance to architectural practice and education. In addition, CPAS published twelve books in Arabic on planning and architecture written by Abdel Baki Ibrahim. It organised training courses for architects, and also four local architectural conferences as well as an international conference entitled "International Conference for Hassan Fathy's Architecture".

The Journal Dizain i Novaia Arhitectura, *Tatarstan*

DINA SATTAROVA

The journal *Dizain i Novaia Arhitectura* (Design and New Architecture) is the only professional publication in the Republic of Tatarstan and in the surrounding region devoted to issues relating to architecture and town planning. The idea of the journal arose from the urgent necessity of illuminating and discussing regional problems affecting architecture in a specialised periodical. The journal was created as a result of the cooperative efforts of experts from numerous fields – architects, art critics, historians, cultural geographers and builders – representing different artistic alliances, organisations and institutes from Tatarstan and Russia. The first issue of the journal appeared in May 1999.

The journal addresses issues such as the formation of an original architectural tradition, the preservation of the heritage of the city, and the development of modern architectural and town planning practices. Issues devoted to specialised subjects such as the millennial anniversary of Kazan, the capital of Tatarstan, and other cities in the republic were also published. These issues have highlighted the unique culture of Tatarstan, which is a result of interactions between traditions and styles from various cultures.

In our journal, we aim to promote aesthetic values in our society, to attract new authors to write on architecture, and to attract new readers and architectural enthusiasts. We have therefore put out a series of publications devoted to the classical architectural heritage of Islam in the region, and also to the new architecture of the republic that is being formed in the spirit of restoring that heritage.

We suffer in Tatarstan from an acute deficiency of professional literature devoted to subjects such as the theory and history of architecture, town planning development and modern construction in the region. We therefore hope that *Dizain i Novaia Arhitectura* will have a positive effect on the development of architecture in the republic and region, as well as enhance the quality of local architectural research. We also hope that our work will promote a consolidation of a professional culture and encourage the integration of this culture into a wider cultural context.

Architectural Publishing in Pakistan

MURTUZA SHIKOH

*A*rchi Times and *Architecture + Interiors* (*A+I*) are Pakistan's sole architectural publications. Consequently, they constitute the only source of professional information about contemporary architecture in the country. What follows are a few comments based on my experiences as publisher and editor of these two magazines.

Archi Times, which is printed in newspaper format (46 x 30 centimetres), is a monthly publication that covers current architectural news, both locally and internationally. It also promotes architects through featuring interviews with them, as well as profiles of their work. We have showcased the work of numerous prominent Pakistani architects who have been practising over the past fifty years. The issues of the publication consequently provide a catalogue that features interviews with local and international architects, and covers news and happenings in the field. In fact, such a compilation will soon appear in book format. It should also be emphasised that, in selecting the works featured in *Archi Times*, we have aimed at creating a platform that presents various architectural ideologies, rather than promoting a single approach to the making of architecture.

The second publication, *A+I*, which is printed in magazine format (23 x 30 centimetres), is the only quarterly magazine in Pakistan that covers local and international architectural, interior design, conservation and landscape projects, and provides a critical analysis of architectural trends taking place in the country. It documents the work of Pakistani architects, both young and old, extending over Pakistan's history of over half a century. The prime objective of *A+I* is to document and emphasise the quality, creativity, sensitivity and innovation found in the work of these architects. It is the first publication to provide a platform for the architects of Pakistan to share their work with other professionals, young architects and students.

These publications have provided me with an excellent opportunity to interact closely with a number of architects. I have found them to be very creative individuals, but also highly sensitive to criticism and with a very low tolerance level for it. We are nonetheless trying to get them to accept and understand architectural criticism, and to convey to them that it can have a positive impact on the creative process.

As a publisher and editor who strongly believes in the value of architectural criticism, I feel I have a responsibility to analyse works of architecture rather than simply describe them in positive terms. Unfortunately, we face hardships in this endeavour. Whenever a critical analysis of an architecturally significant project is published, we face the wrath of architects who are not ready to accept criticism positively. Not only do they express displeasure with our assessment of their work, they also criticise our publications in such a way that discourages our advertisers from continuing to advertise with us, thus leading to financial losses. In our part of the world, no governmental or private sector funding is available to support publications such as ours, and we therefore survive primarily on income from advertising.

Another issue we encounter is what to publish and what to critique. Each individual has his or her own criteria for categorising projects as good or bad examples of architecture. Many criticise the work of others on the basis of their personal likes and dislikes, which makes it difficult to set a common standard for the selection of projects for publication. In our part of the world, all sorts of architecture, both good and bad, exist. We do our best to document the best of what exists. However, we also feel it is our responsibility to present all that is being created. Consequently, a criticism regularly made of us is that we do not publish only good architecture. Our response to this criticism is that we publish what is taking place and what defines the mainstream of architectural production in the country. We intend to continue showcasing the architectural trends taking place in the country. Our readers are globally savvy, and are aware of the latest architectural developments, both local and international. They are therefore able to differentiate quality.

Another difficulty I come across in architectural publishing is in compiling various architectural works. Most of the architects we approach in order to publish their work do not have organised portfolios. This leads to considerable delays in the publishing process, and also affects its quality.

One shortcoming that is present in the writings we publish is that even when a project is analysed, the discourse is limited to the formal characteristics of the project, without any analysis of its social, cultural, economic, physical, or environmental contexts. Moreover, the manner in which criticism is carried out has a strong Western bias, and is not related to local culture or to the local mindset.

I believe that education is the only solution for overcoming these challenges. It is imperative to introduce courses in architectural criticism in Pakistan's schools of architecture in order to achieve a better understanding of the built environment around us and its impact on our society, culture and regional context.

Architectural Criticism and Publishing in Kazakhstan

TIMUR TUREKULOV

The young state of Kazakhstan is witnessing a construction boom. As is the case with numerous other places in the world where similar changes are taking place, this construction boom is not in line with the real needs of the country's cities and their inhabitants. The changes are being influenced primarily by commercial and political forces, rather than social ones, even though such social forces remain to be recognised as important and powerful instruments that are capable of achieving successful and sustainable development.

The new construction taking place in Kazakhstan is in opposition to the country's urban and architectural heritage. While trying to keep up with the latest international architectural achievements, it often ignores the local context and encroaches on historical and traditional areas. The national character of the country's architecture is consequently being threatened. Even though during the Soviet period there was an emphasis on the use of industrial prefabricated construction technologies, attention was given to developing a national identity in architecture. It is true that we are becoming more exposed to the outside world and more integrated with it, and that the available opportunities in terms of financial resources and access to architectural developments taking place internationally are offering new freedoms of expression in architecture. However, we are running the risk of blindly replicating foreign architectural examples as we are not yet prepared to critically address the forces of globalisation.

Such circumstances increase the need for developing a tradition of architectural criticism to help bridge past and future, and to connect architects, constructors and clients together. However, the field of architectural criticism in Kazakhstan remains a new one that has not yet been fully discovered, let alone recognised as part of the professional activities affecting architecture and construction. Rarely does one hear the news or opinions of architects in the media, even though the public is very interested in the building activity taking place in the country. Architectural criticism exists, but only as a verbal exercise, as is the case, for example, at meetings of town planning councils or at project presentations made by architects to city managers and contractors. The discussions that take place there are not accessible to the public since they are not reported in the media, and definitely not published. This creates a huge gap between the makers of architecture and its consumers.

The gap is widening further because of the lack of information published in local languages about international architectural and urban planning practices.

The absence of journalists with a professional architectural background, along with the lack of governmental attention to the subject, aggravates this current situation. Media coverage of architecture is primarily limited to narratives about projects, and to congratulatory notices to architects and clients that appear in newspapers. However, we rarely come across any analysis of projects that addresses their architecture, intentions, or achieved results.

Kumbez, a private magazine established in 1997, is the only architectural magazine to be published in Kazakhstan. This specialised magazine provides a platform for expressing and exchanging ideas and opinions on architecture-related issues among professionals, and at the same time aims at reaching the general public.

The role of photography in this magazine is very important. Photographs are used, often without captions, as a means of expression since architecture is a visual product of human activity that is understood primarily by the human eye. Images communicate to everyone, and provide a universal language that communicates to both professionals and non-professionals. It communicates to the lay public without the need for explanation. Even a photograph that is not taken by a professional photographer may explain a work of architecture better than a written description. Images cannot be a substitute for reality, but do help us achieve a better understanding of buildings and cities. No architectural publication can be successful without photographs, which can provide precise and comprehensive sources of information. With the use of the Internet, photographs may be transmitted easily anywhere around the world. This allows one to stay in touch with the latest developments, and provides a powerful tool for the expression and exchange of ideas.

VI. REGIONAL PERSPECTIVES

Crisis of Modernity and the Lack of Architectural Criticism in the Arab World

MASHARY A. AL-NAIM

Arab societies have been influenced by the process of modernisation, especially in the twentieth century. Traditional societies in the Arab world have been transformed from belonging to isolated regions constituting small, scattered towns and villages to belonging to modern countries with large cities and huge social and economic networks. This has influenced their traditional political, economic and social orders, and has increased the gap between traditional orders and new ones.[1] New ways of thinking, often contradicting previous ones, have come into being within these traditional societies. However, this has not been associated with a clear vision or plan for the modernisation of Arab cities. Cities were modernised with no screening of, or integration with, main intellectual trends. For example, traditional societies are dependent on traditions and customs as codes for organisation, while contemporary modern societies are strongly influenced by rationality. The faith of modern societies is usually based on science, pragmatic reasoning and utilitarianism, while traditional societies tend to believe in the legitimacy of scriptural teaching and traditional norms.[2] This essay tries to analyse current 'reforms' in Arab architectural criticism by diagnosing this division in thought and its impact on contemporary Arab architecture.

Addressing modern Arab cities within the concept of modernisation versus Westernisation will open up the issue of colonisation, which initiated the process of modernisation for most cities in the region. As a result, any attempt to write about modern architecture in Arab cities needs to confront the impact of the Westernisation process that has divided Arab intellectuals into two opposing parties. There are the liberals on the one hand, who encourage and support the process of Westernisation; and the traditionalists on the other, who insist on maintaining traditional Islamic values and preserving the historical morals of Arab societies. Not only has this split in vision and beliefs influenced the physical environment, it has also influenced every single activity in the region over the past two centuries; and it is clear that this conflict will continue in the future. Modern architecture in Arab cities has undoubtedly been influenced by political and intellectual conditions, and any attempt to critique it and write about it should address this debate between liberals and traditionalists.

SOME THOUGHTS ON THE LACK OF ARCHITECTURAL CRITICISM IN THE ARAB WORLD

To begin with, it should be stated that the concept of architectural criticism is not part of the contemporary culture of the Arab mind. In fact, it may be argued that architectural education in the Arab world has failed to build any school of thought in architectural criticism. This is due to a number of reasons. Amongst them is that the philosophy of architectural education in the region has been directed by, and dedicated to, producing governmental employees rather than real practising architects. This is why most architectural departments in Arab universities belong to schools of engineering. This has isolated architecture from current intellectual debates, and is expressed by the fact that architecture (*'imara*) is commonly referred to as engineering (*handasa*), and that an architect (*mi'mar*) is referred to as an engineer (*muhandis*). The aesthetic and human aspects of architecture have therefore become less important than technical ones, and this has consequently pushed architecture away from social and intellectual concerns.

The aforementioned situation has resulted in a state of confusion. The situation has not changed much since the Egyptian ruler Muhammad 'Ali established the first schools that provided architectural education during the first half of the nineteenth century, the *Muhandiskhanas* (based on the Ottoman engineering schools of that time). Even when formal university architectural education was later initiated during the second decade of the twentieth century in Lebanon, during the 1940s in Syria, and during the 1960s in countries including Saudi Arabia and Libya, the situation did not change. This is not to say that the state of architectural education in the region has been the only reason for the lack of development of a tradition of architectural criticism. Another important reason is the confusion between modernisation and Westernisation in the modern Arab mind. The acceptance of Modern architecture in the region has been treated with a level of hesitation because it was a product of the colonial period. This is a very critical issue, and has resulted in isolating both intellectuals and laymen from the physical environment around them. A further reason is the shortage of published books and articles about architecture. Architectural education has not encouraged writing on the field in Arabic. It would also seem that writing about architecture does not receive much attention, and there is no market in the region for it.

In this context, I would like to draw attention to three architectural magazines that faced serious challenges and were forced to cease publication. *Alemara* (*al-'Imara*; Architecture), the Arab world's first architecture magazine, was established by the Egyptian architect Sayyid Kurayyim in Cairo in 1939, and continued publication (with some interruptions) until 1959. *Alam Al Bena* ('*Alam al-Bina'*; The World of Construction) was established in 1980 by Abdel Baki Ibrahim and his partner and brother Hazem Ibrahim through the Centre for Planning and Architectural Studies (CPAS), and continued to be published until 1999. And then there was *Madina*, which was edited by Amr Abdel Kawi and appeared from 1998 until 2001. The only architectural magazine in the region that has survived over a relatively lengthy period is the monthly *Albenaa* ('*al-Bina'*; Building), published in Riyadh.[3] The challenges facing architectural publishing in the region have delayed the evolution of local architectural movements, and, as a result, Arab cities have grown without any critical assessment of their architecture.

While tradition contrasts with modernity, they cannot both exist in isolation of each other. This contrasts with C. B. Wilson's statement that "society cannot be both modern and traditional at the same time".[4] "Strands of tradition", however, may continue in modern societies, even when the society to which they belong has disappeared. We should realise, though, that these strands do not reflect the whole tradition.[5] The view that traditions are able to continue in modern societies may be linked to what Edward Shils suggests when he stresses that the ambiguity and flexibility of traditions enable new concepts to survive and develop. In that sense, traditions

> often possess sufficient ambiguity and hence flexibility to allow innovations to enter without severely disruptive consequences. Then, too, patterns of traditional beliefs (and their accompanying practices) do not form such a rigorously unitary whole; some parts are more affirmative towards modernity, or at least less resistant towards innovation. Many traditional beliefs are not so much objects of zealous devotion to symbols of the past as they are the resultants of a situation without alternatives. Once alternatives become visible and available, what appeared to be an immobile tradition might well yield to a new practice.[6]

Despite the common belief that a society becomes modern only when it totally rejects its traditional sociocultural bonds, continuity of traditions in modern societies is essential. This is not to say that society will be both traditional and modern, but, as Karl Popper explained, tradition emerges as a result of our need for a certain predictability in our social life. In this regard, tradition provides order and regularity in our social environment and provides us with the possibility of communication with each other and with others.[7] Without tradition "there can no longer be reliance on [...] accepted norms".[8] However, "tradition is not a matter of a fixed or given set of beliefs or practices which are handed down or accepted passively".[9] Rather, as Wright has argued, "tradition is very much a matter of present-day politics".[10]

This is not the case in the Arab world, where the impact of traditions on the Arab mind is beyond the idea of 'hybrid' culture, which is composed of traditional and modern aspects; in the Arab world, hybridity tends to be more traditional. Living in the past may be considered part of the cultural problems of this region, which have created over time a kind of segregation between present life and its people. Reciting history and praising a past associated with nostalgic and sentimental feelings have created a trend in architectural writing that looks back to history rather than the present. The result is that criticism has not been part of the decision-making process, and most architectural developments have taken place without the input of intellectual or social revisions. The impact of political conditions cannot be ignored either, where talking about what is taking place in present-day life is often not allowed.

There is no doubt that continuity of traditions or their strands in modern societies can be seen as a sort of internal resistance by people as they attempt to balance deep-rooted values and new ones.

Seyyed Hossein Nasr shares this view, and adds that tradition "is related etymologically to transmission", and contains within the scope of its meaning the idea of "transmission of knowledge, practice, techniques, laws, forms and many other elements of both an oral and written nature".[11] Tradition, in this sense, is seen as a mechanism that has no authority but "forms the most important source of our knowledge and serves as the base of our thought and action".[12] Amos Rapoport defined tradition as a model resulting from the "collaboration of many people over many generations". For him, tradition "has the force of law honored by everyone through collective assent". Therefore, respect for tradition by members of the community gives "collective control", which works as a form of "discipline" for a community.[13]

However, what has taken place in contemporary Arab societies has been very radical. Tradition is still considered of great importance, and most Arabic writings on architecture have addressed the subject of how to revive and maintain traditions. This has directed the writings and studies about architecture to historical issues rather than modern ones that would make the idea of criticism a part of people's daily life. We cannot deny the importance of traditions, but in the case of Arab societies there has been no balance. Living in the past has remained a dominant phenomenon, and there has been no room for any criticism of what is to be built in modern Arab cities. In addition, the political situation has not helped, for most Arab critics find themselves in danger if they criticise what is taking place around them, and the only door open to them has been that of the past and history.

THE DILEMMA OF WESTERNISATION AND THE NEED FOR ARCHITECTURAL CRITICISM
It is clear that it is not possible for any architectural criticism to survive in such a political climate. This was especially the case during the 1960s, 1970s and 1980s. However, Arab cities have undergone rapid urban growth, which has been associated with rapid socio-economic change.[14] As is the case with other developing countries, the conflict in the Arab world is between borrowed elements, which are largely physical, and inherited elements, which are mostly values and beliefs.[15] This has produced numerous social problems for the urbanisation of the Arab city. An almost complete urban transformation has taken place in Arab cities during the last century. It is debatable whether this physical change caused social change or vice versa.[16] What is clear is that an obvious contradiction has appeared in Arab society between tradition and modernity. Thus, the ability of the contemporary built environment to meet the cultural demands of Arab society may be questioned.

There is both confusion in the distinction between Westernisation and modernisation and a worldwide phenomenon – largely due to Western writers – of frequently defining any modernisation process as an adoption of Western cultural, economic and political models.[17] Orrin Klapp, for example, indicates that the problem of identity is the price that developing societies should pay for technological advancement. He writes:

It is ironical to see underdeveloped countries marching into the future as though they were going to receive the blessing of technology and abundance without the price of self-doubt that seems to go with them. Probably they would say: "Give us the tractors first and we'll be glad to take on the luxury of worrying about identity problems".[18]

Vincent Costello also discussed Western influences on Middle Eastern countries in the second half of the twentieth century.[19] Generally, Western influences have developed a desire to maintain local culture all over the world.[20] Besim Hakim shares these views and indicates that three decades after World War II a conflict between traditional and modern values has spread across the Arabic-Islamic world, which has brought the issue of identity in the built environment to centre stage.[21]

The major argument presented in Western studies on modernisation stresses that non-Western societies become modern only when they interact with Western societies, especially when they are "invaded, defeated and exploited by the West". What is clear is that the West is, "evidently, a name always associating itself with those regions, communities and peoples that appear politically or economically superior to other regions, communities and peoples".[22]

It is necessary here to clarify that an overlap, if not confusion, between the concepts of 'modernisation' and 'Westernisation' is widely found in non-Western societies. However, it is Western scholars who originally generated this misinterpretation. Many Western scholars attributed the modernisation process to Western culture. This can be clearly understood from Shils' statement that "'modern' means being Western without the onus of dependence on the West".[23] This view is shared by Dankwart Rustow when he states that "modernization began in Europe in the Renaissance and spread overseas in the wake of Europe's expansion".[24] Also, when discussing European cultural identity, Jorge Larrain states that "this identity conceived of place [Europe] as the centre where history was being made and it was able to place and recognize everybody else as peripheral".[25]

It is assumed in much of the literature that as earlier modernisation took place in Western societies, it is somehow an intrinsically Western process. However, one may easily clarify the difference between modernisation as a process that may occur at any time and in any society, and Westernisation, which appeared in the colonial era, and by which those societies governed by Western governments were forced to adopt Western ways of living.

Modernisation, in that sense, "is very much a Westernization process; a process which depends largely on imitation rather than on innovation".[26] It is a term applied only to non-Western traditional societies, the modernisation efforts of which have been judged by Western criteria. This has meant that for any society to be modern, it should adopt a Western model for modernisation. Paul Recoeur criticises this tendency when he indicates the impact of universalisation on local cultures. He asserts that the phenomenon of universalization, while being an advancement of mankind, at the same time constitutes a sort of subtle destruction, not only of traditional cultures, which might not be an irreparable wrong, but also of what I shall call for the time being the creative nucleus of great civilizations and great culture, that nucleus on the basis of which we interpret life, what I shall call in advance the ethical and mythical nucleus of mankind.[27]

This view is supported by Rapoport when he criticises the impact of Westernisation on other cultures. He states that there

is a danger in applying western concepts, which represent only one choice among the many possible, to the problems of other areas, instead of looking at them in terms of local ways of life, specific needs, and ways of doing things.[28]

Modernity as a philosophical concept is widely integrated with the concept of Westernisation in the Arab world. These two concepts have been ambiguously connected in both literature and in people's minds, thus increasing the resistance to physical change in the contemporary Arab city. Thus, the issue of identity has risen as a result of the association between the process of modernisation and that of Westernisation. It is thus argued here that the need for identity in the Arab world is widely associated with the threat that people feel as a result of the rapid changes that traditional societies have experienced in the last two centuries.

It is clear from the above that we misinterpret the process of modernisation. The lack of criticism has deepened this misinterpretation and has created cultural barriers between the Arab world and the West. Architectural criticism has not been a priority, and consequently this has isolated architecture from its cultural and social contexts. The following discussion tries to postulate the position that we should find ways to bring architecture back to its social and cultural contexts by activating and encouraging architectural criticism in publishing and also as an educational tool.

ATTEMPTS AT REFORM: *ALBENAA* MAGAZINE AS AN EXAMPLE

Albenaa, an Arabic-language architectural magazine published in Riyadh, Saudi Arabia, was established by Ibrahim Aba Al-Khail in 1978. At the date of writing this essay, the magazine is publishing its 189th issue. It is the only architectural magazine in the Arab world that has been published continuously over the past quarter of a century. This continuity in publication has enabled *Albenaa* to document a very large number of buildings designed and constructed in Arab cities. The philosophy of the magazine is to publish in each issue a special section on an architectural subject that would end up covering most well-known architects and buildings in the Arab world. From its inception, *Albenaa*'s main goal has been to develop architectural consciousness about contemporary Arab architecture. Therefore, over the last quarter of a century, thousands of buildings and hundreds of articles have been published in the magazine, which has been of considerable use to architectural students and professionals in the region.

I started working with *Albenaa* as senior editor in August 2000. Since then, I have tried to direct the magazine to give increasing attention to criticism, and have initiated new ways of commenting on projects, writing critical essays about local and regional architecture, and interviewing prominent Arab architects. The magazine's vision was developed and redirected towards architectural criticism. Accordingly, we have published special issues about Arab cities (Riyadh, Cairo, Dubai, Kuwait, Beirut, and so on). In these issues, we made an attempt to reconnect architecture with its cultural, social, political and technical contexts. The magazine has also tried to create a network for Arab writers on architecture. There is no documentation of architectural drawings in the region, and few of its architects have made any efforts at publishing their work. By developing this network, we can reduce the time needed for documenting and identifying visions regarding local environments in the Arab world. The attempt has been successful, and the results have been wonderful. We now believe there is at last a chance to establish a local tradition of architectural criticism.

We recently developed the idea of conducting a critical study of contemporary architecture in the Arab world with the aim of establishing a tradition of comparative architectural criticism. We started in 2002 (issue nos. 146 and 147) to ask authors to write critical essays about contemporary Arab architecture. In these two issues, we published a special section regarding the paradigm shifts in Arab architecture defining four milestones over the past two centuries. Later, at the end of 2005 and early 2006 (issue nos. 182, 183, 184 and 185), we published four special sections regarding Arab architecture, contributed by a number of writers from Egypt, Syria, Algeria, Palestine, Saudi Arabia, Kuwait, Sudan, Jordan, Tunisia, Algeria, Bahrain and the United Arab Emirates. Our plan now is to continue building up a body of critical knowledge about contemporary Arab architecture that, in the future, may help redirect architectural practice in the region.

CONCLUSION

To recapitulate, the development of a tradition of architectural criticism in the Arab world has been negatively affected by educational and political problems. On the one hand, architectural education has not been designed to produce critics, thus ending up with a weak intellectual environment in which there are no publications, writers, or readers. On the other, the political situation has prevented any critique of decisions affecting the cities of the Arab world and their architecture. There are also reasons inherent in the nature of criticism, which the architects themselves do not encourage (the only words they want to hear is "your work is the best"). Another reason for the lack of development of a tradition of architectural criticism in our part of the world is a cultural one, and relates to the confusion between modernisation and Westernisation, which strengthens the feeling that modern Arab architecture was a product of the colonial era. However, there is still hope that this dark scene will change. For example, *Albenaa* has tried over the last three decades to establish a sort of school of thought in Arab architectural criticism. There is still a lot of work that needs to be done to fix the damage and to bridge the gap between architectural criticism and construction activities in the Arab world.

[1] See George A. Lipsky, *Saudi Arabia: Its People, Its Society, Its Culture*, HRF Press, New Haven, Conn. 1959.

[2] See Daniel Lerner, *The Passing of Traditional Society: Modernizing the Middle East*, Free Press, New York 1958, pp. 48–49; and Edward Shils, *Political Development in the New States*, Mouton, The Hague 1962. Shils indicates that traditional societies are "attached to beliefs and rules which guided past practices, and which are regarded as guides to right practice in the present. The attachment to these beliefs is firmer or more intense than it is in modern societies, and it is more widely shared throughout the society" (p. 31).

[3] *Albenaa* will be discussed in more detail later in this essay.

[4] Cited in Chao-Ching Fu, "Regional Heritage and Architecture - A Critical Regionalist Approach to a New Architecture for Taiwan", Ph.D. dissertation, University of Edinburgh, 1990, p. 15.

[5] Ibid.

[6] Shils, *Political Development* cit., p. 32.

[7] Karl Popper, "Towards a Rational Theory of Tradition", in his *The Growth of Scientific Knowledge*, Harper and Row, New York 1968, pp. 120–135.

[8] Amos Rapoport, *House Form and Culture*, Prentice Hall, Englewood Cliffs, New Jersey 1969, p. 6.

[9] David Morley and Kevin Robins, *Spaces of Identity*, Routledge, London 1995, p. 47.

[10] Cited in ibid.

[11] Seyyed Hossein Nasr, *Knowledge and the Sacred*, Edinburgh University Press, Edinburgh 1981, p. 67.

[12] Saleh Al-Hathloul, "Tradition, Continuity, and Change in the Physical Environment: The Arab-Muslim City", Ph.D. dissertation, Massachusetts Institute of Technology, 1981, p. 254.

[13] Rapoport, *House Form and Culture* cit., p. 6.

[14] See Geoffrey Payne, *Urban Housing in the Third World*, Leonard Hill, London 1977, p. 3.

[15] Ali al-Jarbawi, "Modernism and Secularism in the Arab Middle East", Ph.D. dissertation, University of Cincinnati, 1981, p. 33.

[16] Behavioural-environmental studies have addressed three views regarding the impact of the physical environment on people's behaviour, including environmental determinism, environmental possibilism and environmental probablism. Environmental determinism insists on the deterministic nature of the built environment on human behaviour. Possibilism argues that the physical environment "provides possibilities and constraints within which people make choices based on other, mainly cultural, criteria". Probabilism suggests that the physical environment provides "possibilities for choice and is not determining, but that some choices are more probable than others in given physical settings". See Amos Rapoport, *Human Aspects of Urban Form*, Pergamon Press, Oxford 1977, p. 2; and Maurice Broady, "Social Theory in Architectural Design", in *Arena - The Architectural Association Journal*, 81, January 1966, pp. 149–154.

[17] See S. N. Eisenstadt, *Modernization: Protest and Change*, Prentice-Hall, Englewood Cliffs, New Jersey 1966. He writes: "Historically, modernization is the process of change towards these types of social, economic and political systems that have developed in Western Europe and North America from the seventeenth century to the nineteenth and twentieth centuries to the South American, Asian and African countries" (p. 1). See also Payne, *Urban Housing* cit., pp. 13–20.

[18] Orrin Klapp, *Collective Search for Identity*, Holt, Rinehart and Winston, New York 1969, p. 4. He illustrates several examples from non-Western societies (Japan and India), in which he explains how these societies become confused about their identities. These societies stressed traditions as a refuge from a sense of rottenness. (pp. 15–16). In the case of the Arab world, N. Daniel discusses the concept of "Westernization must mean modernization". He indicates the resistance of Arab societies to modernisation due to its Western origin. According to him, "Arabs [...] can hope to modernize in a way characteristic of their own cultural history. Their profound resentment at a hundred years of political, economic and cultural interference will ensure that they will take Western technology with a minimum of Western ideas..." See N. Daniel, "Westernization in the Arab World", in Michael Adams (ed.), *The Middle East*, Anthony Blond, London 1971, pp. 516–525.

[19] See Vincent F. Costello, *Urbanization in the Middle East*, Cambridge University Press, Cambridge 1977.

[20] For example, in Japan it was expected that "economic transformation necessitates a transformation in society which shifts Japan inevitably closer to the ideals, values and ways of the West. In due course, the homogenizing spread of Western culture will absorb the remnants of an Eastern tradition [...] [What happened is] that the distinctiveness of the Japanese outlook on life still persists and that, in the minds of ordinary folk, things have changed less radically than crude social and material manifestations might suggest." See Michael Jeremy and M. E. Robinson, *Ceremony and Symbolism in the Japanese Home*, University of Hawaii Press, Honolulu 1989, p. xi.

[21] Besim Hakim, "The 'Urf' and Its Role in Diversifying the Architecture of Traditional Islamic Cities", in *Journal of Architectural and Planning Research*, 11: 2, 1994, pp. 108–127.

[22] Morley and Robins, *Spaces of Identity* cit., p. 159.

[23] Shils, *Political Development* cit., p. 10.

[24] Dankwart Rustow, *A World of Nations: Problems of Political Modernization*, Brookings Institution, Washington D.C. 1967, p. 1.

[25] Jorge Larrain, *Ideology and Cultural Identity: Modernity and the Third World Presence*, Polity Press, Cambridge 1994, p. 141.

[26] Al-Jarbawi, "Modernism and Secularism" cit., p. 3.

[27] Cited in Kenneth Frampton, *Modern Architecture: A Critical History*, Thames and Hudson, London 1980, p. 314.

[28] Rapoport, *House Form and Culture* cit., p. 129. Also, Alan Lomax and Norman Berkowitz had criticised this phenomenon when they said: "Man's total heritage of life-styles can contribute to the future, without giving precedence any longer to the European social and aesthetic practices that accompanied the rise of industry". See Alan Lomax with Norman Berkowitz, "The Evolutionary Taxonomy of Culture", in *Ekistics*, 36: 213, August 1973, pp. 77–84.

An Agenda for Architectural Journalism and Criticism in Iran

DARAB DIBA

Can architecture be isolated from world events? Can it be evaluated or shaped in isolation from international trends and the interactions of science, economy, or politics? Today, due to compressed time-space notions, the request and need for swift contacts between communities have become pressing. The communications media has allowed for a considerable awareness of events in other countries, and many people now draw their dynamism from cultural interactions.

While a major part of the world is still caught in poverty, injustice and insecurity, the common factors of these countries for global coexistence are a precarious status quo of established forces, and acquiring the rights of freedom and knowledge is not at all taken for granted. The wars of authority and power have become wars of interests, and the new interconnected world economy is formulated by today's superpowers. An unbalanced international economic system is still firmly applied through the existing gap between regions with dire economic needs and prosperous industrialised countries. Deprived communities remain deprived, and only enigmatic issues motivate ethical values, which remain in isolated islands of cultural discourses, promulgating only hopes and speeches, or becoming tools and excuses for political or ideological autocratic rule.

The closure of the twentieth century has been accompanied by a reversion to the wholeness of the world and of history, in whose long-term waves one may perhaps seek to surmise a new theory, which of course reveals no new truth, and only endeavours at studying and furthering present limits.

Our world today is facing new imperative requirements that call for a revised assessment of our perceptions. In an age of communication and extensive exchange, the appreciation of diversity may lead to a wider acceptance of tolerance. Identity issues must be linked to global welfare and to considerations for attaining means for achievements. At that level, while preserving all cultural values, progressive concepts may become the instrumental attainment of science and reason, and of a more civilised status. In that podium, architecture, as a universal expression, represents a general assessment of cultural realisation. In theoretical analysis, in criticism, or in journalism, the compendium of rhetorical thinking gives only an outlook regarding the diversity of views shaped by the nature of the discipline itself, which may not be easily deciphered, leaving the field open to all kinds of dialectic interpretations and dilemma.

A visionary architecture must embody imagination in action and must dramatise the creative process through the convergence of the universality of space, leaving formal expressions in the shades of the essentials. The humanistic role of architecture entails the convergence of all facts, laws and events, and therefore, for the sake of achieving any sense of unity, should lead to their integration.

We must admit that our task is much harder today, because the social and economic forces affecting the shape of human societies and their interactions are becoming more and more complicated, while political and economic decisions impinge on the moral dimension. Accordingly, the humanity, for which many thinkers have fought in the course of history, is often relegated to lowest priorities of idealistic floating consciences. We have to realise that globalisation does not mean losing oneself and one's regional wealth, and does not imply cultural radicalism and uniformity; each nation still has to make great efforts in this complex world to contribute. This, of course, calls for freedom of access to information, freedom of expression, and freedom of communication, or, in other words, the evolution of a paradigm that is likely to serve man's development in some way. In today's world, views and theories concerning architectural design and the identity of buildings are highly complicated issues. The time of absolute confidence in the Modern movement of the early twentieth century has passed. At the other extreme, the pluralistic views of the present could lead to a straight individualistic mannerism or peculiar stages of eclecticism in a period of high hybridisation. These formal architectural plays, combined with esoteric hybrid reasoning, even with the assumption of freeing space and extending boundaries, often lie to a reality where experiment justifies the character of their creation.

When discussions about deconstruction began a few decades ago, we became conscious of a dynamic new vision based on the analysis of problems and the rejection of dogmatism, empiricism and historical categorical philosophical rulings. Deconstruction was an attempt to free philosophy from its built constraints, the 'takings-for-granted' that for centuries have stultified thinking. Jacques Derrida's issue of "logocentrism" applied the belief that one cannot get to the bottom of things through logic, rational argument, or revelation, and that only investigation could gain a conceptual approach for things and thoughts. Through that path, we oversaw all those who destroyed "the myth of the given": Ludwig Wittgenstein, Martin Heidegger, and others who proved there are not, and cannot be, "ultimate Obstacles" to the journey of knowledge. Generally speaking, through scientific inquiry, we became conscious of efforts devoted to the discovery of new conceptual horizons, which the reflections of Derrida, Paul Ricoeur, Roland Barthes, Michel Foucault, Gilles Deleuze, and many other new philosophers greatly clarified, allowing these concepts to be analysed, and their constituent components identified. Therefore, if a bridge truly existed, is it still strong in our perception of the general criteria for the evaluation of life?

THE IRANIAN CONTEXT

Let us see what has happened in Iran in the face of globalised phenomena and views, and current architectural trends. The debates and conflicts regarding contemporary Iranian architecture are still ongoing, and the search for an identity is still vacillating between a nostalgic parody of the past and the import of Western models. Our life, as Iranian architects, always searching for the ideal substantial essence, is an inexorable challenge of delicate counterbalances, where issues of authenticity are framed by global universal views.

Innovative and sustainable for centuries, architecture declined in the twentieth century with the advent of colonial and imperialistic politics, and with the influx of oil wealth. To that, problems such as incompetent local authorities, poor national planning, a stagnating economy and autocratic and repressive regimes also helped through the years to dismantle the pre-existing civil social context.

Today, our evaluation of ourselves and of our design production leads us to widen the meanings of our substance so as to capture the universal values in which architecture, as a receptacle, may comprehend other disciplines in which perennial qualities remain omnipresent: liberty, equality, efficiency, development, technology, authenticity and tolerance. In fact, architecture cannot be disassociated from its ideological and political context, and notions of identity and culture must be related to the present; a present in which an enlightened mainstream of intelligence and comprehension unites a recollection of cultures and civilisations where identity is perceived more within the context of sameness rather than difference.

Today, in the electronic age, thousands of young people are contributing, with talent and courage, to improving the human environment through implementing progressive values and through challenging the misery and the pressure of obsolete dogmas. The new generation exhibits a new approach that incorporates a diversified architectural language. Partly under the influence of globalisation, and through its intertwined histories and cultural imaginations, this generation is aiming for a more universal architecture, feeling no compulsion to seek a synthesis of the international and local, but recreating new networks of information and knowledge, and transforming past exclusions into new inclusive subjective data.

Maybe we need to identify new ways of thinking, a mental scope where humanity transcends the inner content of architectural expressions and aesthetics. It is time to connect our views to real sciences, to new times, and to the essence of a new emerging substantial world. Through this path, our participation must leave behind all formalistic past and schizophrenic nostalgia so as to embrace the wholeness of the spiritual challenges of the modern world.

However, the eternal question remains as to why a country with such a rich and unique cultural heritage, and with so many concerned people, remains trapped in this state of mediocrity. It seems that any conceptual knowledge-base must extend notions of performance literacy, linking society to various other disciplines of human thought. Architecture is not an exact science. Therefore, how can we persist in reducing it through singular and definitive process analyses of positive evaluation? The good and the bad sometimes become brothers in arms for an unsolved equation of perception, while values may float in the relative disparate complex subtleties of the mind.

Even if we know that the coexistence of art and society is not an easy one; even if the problem remains that of conservative absolutism of a self-proclaimed establishment of rules, our responsibility, as architects, is to challenge the different institutionalised layers of the professional realm. As artists, this task involves allowing ourselves complete freedom. Criticism must deal with the basic structures of society, liberating the displays of opportunities and views, whereas the content could become a metaphor for an iconographic image of social justice and enhanced liberty.

As architects, who prefer diagrams, sketches and doodles to abstract ideas and values, do we have to sketch the answer to believe the platform? Do we have to remain in our dreams of factual amnesia? Shall we not overthrow the mediocrity of a ruling demagogic populism, re-aiming at the installation of some new progressive aesthetics for the sake of a new regeneration? It seems that we have to upgrade and revise processes and matters so as to promote new ideas, and leave aside the bureaucratic, conservative status quo.

Willingly or not, with the advent of new digital tools, globalisation and the extraordinary flux of all kinds of information, we are witnessing a transfer in cultural preference which creates a tremendous shift in architectural evaluation. With this new pluralistic paradigm comes the end of a straightforward Cartesian pursuit of uniformity and generalised exactitude.

Sometimes, for the sake of the journey, it is the mad who discover, in the middle of nowhere, the unfolded lands of our spiritual perception. Through globalisation, the new world view did in fact change our concentration on the specific to the unspecific, creating an interactive understanding of older rationalist progressions of the new poetics of dematerialisation of the actual world. It is an emerging desire for sensibilities and intelligences outside the slipstream of convention, rules and categorical validation that initiates paths of intricacies and variables of new substances. Non-linearity appears as the open sky for comprehensive discovery, where figures stand at the crossroads of many a world view and evaluative social sustainability, and where architecture remains torn between a thousand parameters of framed matrices. Furthermore, following Derrida and Foucault, running through Deleuze's rhizomes, or learning from the spiritual vision of the thirteenth-century Persian poet and teacher of Sufism Mawlana Jalal al-Din al-Rumi, a formal critique is always a good idea that can transfer perennial values.

The rhetoric of cultural dislocation begs the question of how complex things really are. Architectural hermeneutics and the cushy sense of ideological quests, through critical acceptance, are now an integral part of our everyday professional life. Everything seems blurred, even if sometimes we feel nostalgia for once having been people of intelligence. Today, as we are more willing to deal with potential consistence, we have to theorise our prismatic flow of hybridity, even if longing for a lost authenticity, and even if the road is not very clear or is obscured by shadows.

Each man represents a road toward himself
Each man carries the vestiges of his birth
All of us come in at the same door
But each of us strives toward his own destiny
That is why every man's story is important, eternal
But every man is more than just himself
He also represents the Unique
The significant point at which the world's phenomena intersect

Where is the life we have lost in knowledge
Where is the knowledge we have lost in ignorance
The cycle of heaven
Brings us farther from the Truth and nearer to dust

Where are the memories of our heritage
Idea, motion, and creation come in silence
Like a sparrow
Something akin to a new humanity
Where all end begins

I became an architect to build a house beside the woods
So that I could hear you singing
And love was all beginning
Fare thee well my nightingale
It was long ago I found you
Now all your songs of beauty fail
The forest closes round you
Tho' you are singing somewhere still
I can no longer hear you

You walk into my room
With simple kindness
And solitude of strength
It took you years to cross
The line of self-defence

From our passage to Kuwait
From all the words
The sharing joys of freedom
Our hate from politics and imposed poverty

O, Lord
You sent me here
Breaking things
I can't repair[1]

FIVE NOTES ON ARCHITECTURE IN IRAN
Note 1: the state of architectural production
What is the present situation of architecture and architects in Iran? Has a relatively satisfactory stage been reached? Without a doubt, this is not the case. Contemporary Iranian architecture remains in a state of crisis.

High-density architectural production, maximal exploitation of built areas, commercialism and speculation in construction, the lack of coherent general planning, and wanton population growth have all resulted in cities like Tehran with twelve million inhabitants, in which spatial quality has declined, and incoherence, anxiety, as well as traffic, air and sound pollution have reached unacceptable levels. In such a context, necessary qualities such as urban spatial quality and reminiscent human environments are no more perceptible. Through uncontrolled development, the formation of architecture and cities without much regard for human and environmental criteria has brought about the present chaos, and correcting this situation will be a most difficult endeavour.

Iran's architecture and urban planning are afflicted with various difficulties, some of which are mentioned above, but other factors and shortcomings must not be forgotten either. These include a lack of professional awareness; the disarray of the labour market; an unstable economy; the inexistence of an effective and operational institute or order of architects; the supervision of governmental ministries on issues of ethics; financial corruption; national managerial and financial disorganisation; governmental turmoil; the lack of effective social welfare institutions; the predominance of middlemanship; inept construction regulations; the lack of architectural quality control, aesthetics and assessment; shortsighted building codes that allow developers to go beyond maximum allowable built-up areas and building heights for a fee; popular nouveau riche taste; poor detailing and finishing; sub-standard materials; inexperienced manpower; floating schedules; and other social, economic and political problems that prevent this profession from reaching and attaining an acceptable level.

Note 2: a brief history of architectural journalism

During the 1960s, when no real architectural journals existed, *Honar va Memari* (Art and Architecture) was launched by Abdolhamid Eshragh, covering contemporary world architecture, and presenting Iranian architects and artists. Some two decades later, with the absence of any real architectural coverage in the press, Reza Rezai-Rad, through perseverance and through depending on his own means, published *Memari va Shahrsazi* (Architecture and Urbanism), which very soon became the only discussion platform in print for the profession.

Parallel to that, during the 1990s, another architect, Seyyed Reza Hashemi, in collaboration with Soheila Beski, used the magazine *Abadi* (Development), first published in the late 1980s by the Ministry of Housing and Urban Development, to promote various issues relating to the built environment. In the same vein, also during the 1990s, *Memar* was published and soon became an important source documenting architectural events inside and outside Iran. In about the same period, Hossein Soltanzadeh, a dedicated architect and researcher, launched *Memari va Farhang* (Architecture and Culture), which opened a wider range of interdisciplinary issues and social topics. In 2001, Mohammad Reza Jodat published *Memari Iran* (Iranian Architecture). These were followed by publications including *Memari va Rayaneh* (Architecture and Computer) and *Sharestan*.

Today in Iran we have several magazines and journals of architecture and urban planning. However, a link must exist between these publications and architectural production, which remains rather average and often sub-standard in terms of conception, finishing, technology and construction. In fact, the context in which architects function remains a difficult one, and architectural production in the country has yet to reach its potential, even though a relative state of freedom of expression exists.

Note 3: procedural issues relating to architectural publishing

Authorisations and publishing permissions for magazines and journals (and print publications in general) in Iran are issued by the Ministry of Culture and Islamic Guidance. The procedure for obtaining publishing licenses may take several months, and includes an examination of the credentials of the applicant (professional and social) and of other submitted application documents. Scientific journals are subject to less surveillance and control, leaving their writers with a relatively wider margin of freedom. Due to a diverse and complex set of issues and shortcomings, a spontaneous liberty of expression (and professional criticism) has taken place. In the private non-governmental sector, the major source of income for publications comes from advertising.

Note 4: authorities and professional organisations relating to architectural practice
Architecture and urban planning activities and practices are supervised by three main governmental authorities: the Ministry of Housing and Urban Development, the Ministry of Plan and Budget (former Sazman Barnameh), and municipalities.

The main professional organisations relating to architecture are the Engineering Order of the Ministry of Housing and Urban Development, the Syndicate of Consulting Architects and Planners (non-governmental), and the Consulting Engineers and Architects Society (non-governmental).

There is little coordination between these bodies, with each immersed in its own problems and priorities, thus lacking any social management consensus. Differences and difficulties concerning the practice and production of architecture are hardly put forward through a structured dialogue between the private sector, the Syndicate, or the Architects Society and public governmental authorities, which remain the strong decision-making body. Issues relating to regulations, aesthetics, fees, practice, quality control and human environmental theories remain too often locked in a state of intellectual discourse. A strong national independent institute of architects, as part of civil society and liberal professional practice, remains non-existent.

Note 5: schools of architecture
Iran has over forty schools of architecture. The three major schools of architecture and urban planning (Daneshkadeh Memari va Shahrsazi) are in Tehran University, Shahid Beheshti University and Elmo-Sanat (Iran University of Science and Technology). Islamic Azad University is another important institution, with several schools of architecture spread throughout the country. After the Revolution, a uniform programme was established that was deemed more in tune with the country's cultural heritage. However, this programme lacks any serious philosophical, theoretical, social, or environmental basis. The different trends and contextual identities that may differentiate one school from the other have also been somewhat neglected.

A complete reform of architectural education seems urgent in order to enhance new scientific views and universal issues linked to the improvement of the discipline.

---

[1] Darab Diba, "Ending Notes / The End of the Story ", in *Bitter Searching of the Heart: In Tribute to Mowlana, Hermann Hesse, T. S. Eliot, Carl Andersen and L. Cohen*, unpublished poem.

Emerging Architectural Journalism: An Indian Experience

SUNEET PAUL

Globalisation has led to a reasonable exposure to the architecture of different cultures. At the international level, architects are designing structures everywhere, breaking regional boundaries. Architectural journalism has moved further to the forefront. Criticism has gained a wider relevance. No doubt an exciting phase for critics and architectural journalism. Well, as we all realise, the purpose of criticism in architectural journalism is not to condemn or eulogise, but to analyse critically pros and cons, and lead to newer dimensions. Criticism ideally should get behind the work's apparent originality and expose its ideological framework. It is meant to have a base of a careful appraisal or judgement.

Criticism requires an object, which gets recast in a new light. Every individual in his own right is a critic. But he becomes a professional and chiselled one when he achieves a constructive focus and an unbiased approach to balance his judgement. Architectural criticism becomes all the more challenging because what we are dealing with is not quantifiable. The qualitative aspects of this endeavour add dynamism to the writing. It is here that sensitivity to rationalisation comes to the forefront. Criticism in architecture would always be more useful if it addressed the future, keeping the past in mind.

Researchers and critics have also given newer meanings and newer 'isms', and have added newer vocabularies, to design. Amongst the different categories in which academicians have slotted criticism, the interpretative type can be the most exciting. The critic here, with his imagination, creates an image as perceived by himself. The judgmental type of writing can be more complex as it involves the act of evaluating against a standard. Critical analysis is often more productive when it goes with the times. Criticism has to be based on the brief, the client, the end-user, the cultural context and relevance, and of course the subjectivity of the critic. Individual preferences still have to be out-shadowed by the bigger picture. Criticism requires a framework and a structure. A critic needs to have a point of view and to be more accountable, first to himself or herself, and then to the reader.

Reflecting on the Indian scenario, authentic architectural criticism in India is now putting down roots. The slant all along has been more towards documentation and descriptive writing, which also has its relevance. Architectural writing in the country is gathering momentum. There has been a significant increase in the publication of design and architectural magazines. Architectural journalism now is providing a fruitful connection between professionals, the people and the construction industry. My experience in editing two premier design magazines of Media Transasia India in Delhi has told me that nothing can be thrust in the throat of the end-user. Our readers today are more knowledgeable, more exposed to international trends, and more demanding of personalised solutions. Their expectation levels are high, and they are fishing for more in-depth analytical wavelengths. In the Indian context, the diversity in architecture is huge, which makes it adventurous and yet complex for critics to focus on a specific stream of evolution. Creativity here is magnified in scale and is more contextualised regionally. Philosophies, ideologies and sensitivities governing New York or Berlin may not necessarily be appreciated or even relevant in such a context.

The fast track metamorphosis in the industry and people's life styles has made market forces equally more extracting. The mantra is that instead of fighting market forces, architectural journalism has to carry them along. In order to have an impact on the profession and society, it will have to represent all facets linked to architecture. The critics in such circumstances have to bring in more responsibility-linked vibrancy.

The architectural profession too has to become responsive in this exercise of architectural journalism and criticism in order to gain a constructive role in society. Architects have to show more maturity in accepting criticism, and accepting it positively. They need to become more interactive with society's aspirations. Rather than wearing blinkers and creating an ego-linked divide, a more down-to-earth approach is desired. The basics have to be revived. And in this campaign, editors of newspapers and general magazines too have to play a role. Documentation of real estate developments cannot really be presented as architectural writing.

We at *a+d* (*Architecture+Design*) journal/magazine of India, which primarily focuses on professional practice and the construction industry, have attempted to act as a platform that applauds creativity. The members of our target audience, which includes architects, students, industry representatives and lay readers, have experienced greater synergies generated by interactive informal sessions on varied themes related to architecture. We have also initiated awards for celebrating intelligent architecture, as well as focused industry players and talented students. These efforts have undoubtedly allowed the architectural community and the building industry to understand each other better. Our aim has been to act as a cohesive channel to break the ice at different levels. This is our response to changing competitive demands, and we have been successful to a large extent in this endeavour while still retaining our focus.

Regional Reflections: Indonesia

BUDI A. SUKADA

Architectural criticism is not a new enterprise within the discourse of Indonesian architecture. Dutch architects practising in the country initiated a debate during the 1930s about the necessity of establishing a new building style that expressed a local identity that was sensitive to the country's architectural heritage, but nonetheless acknowledged the influences of Modern architecture. Attempts by some of them to establish what they identified as a "modern Indonesian building style" (*Indische moderne bouwenstijl*) however came under strong attack by those who preferred to adopt Modern Dutch European vocabularies, and who took on the position that the monuments of the past had no value. The central issue regarding this architectural debate, therefore, was whether architects in Indonesia should disregard the past or incorporate it into their designs.

By the middle of the twentieth century, the outcome of this debate was settled in favour of complete reliance on the architecture of Modernism. For the next three decades, the mainstream of building design among Indonesian architects was to be influenced heavily by the tenets of Modern architecture, as was their education and training. In this environment, architectural critics were believed to be unnecessary. What was needed most in this period was the knowledge and skills required for applying new technologies of building materials and engineering in order to master the aesthetics of the vocabularies of architectural Modernism as expressed in Kenneth Frampton's notion of "Productivism", which had been applied successfully in numerous parts of the world.[1] Accordingly, Indonesian schools of architecture taught the history of architecture merely as a form of general knowledge according to which the past is of no relevance to the present. In fact, the history of architecture course offered in the architectural curricula of Indonesian universities was an elective one with only a few credit hours.

It seems that the first instance regarding the development of any form of architectural criticism among Indonesian architects took place in 1981, when students of architecture in the country held their second national meeting in Jakarta, and expressed strong dissatisfaction with the works being carried out at that time by senior Indonesian architects. They initially launched a manifesto that questioned the current direction of Indonesian architectural discourse and also the recent works of Indonesian architects. This was followed by official visits by student delegates to a number of these senior architects in order to express their disappointment with their work.

This student manifesto emerged as the main subject of discussion at the national convention of the Indonesian Institute of Architects that took place the following year. The title of the seminar that was held in connection with the convention was "Searching for the Identity of Indonesian Architecture", and this was accompanied by discussions concerning how to address this issue from the perspectives of methodology and practice. Regarding methodology, the proposed agenda was to look at the subject matter from Charles Jencks' approach regarding the "language of architecture",[2] or Bruce Allsopp's view of the so-called "format theory".[3] In the first proposal, it was debated whether Indonesian architecture is a signifier or a collection of signified objects that could be manipulated by architects to come up with a new kind of architecture representing national identity. The second proposal suggested a matrix consisting of sources that represent an Indonesian identity and that might be comprehensively reworked and interpreted by architects.

Regarding the subject of practice, many ideas were put forward. Some suggested adopting the principle of "*Soko Guru*", the four main posts typical of Javanese buildings, to become the starting point in designing new structures that represent modern Indonesian architecture, while others proposed emphasising national features such as the "*Bahasa Indonesia*" (Indonesian language), tropical climate, wet and dry seasons, as well as building traditions. Some ideas that may be described as naive, sentimental and romantic were also put forward, such as the utilisation of Indonesian literature. No significant results came out of the seminar since the ideas presented were all speculative and without any theoretical basis.

The next national convention, which was held in 1984, did not provide any progress regarding these issues. The main topic of the convention was architectural education in Indonesia, and the workshop that was held in connection with the convention supported the status quo according to which courses on the history and theory of architecture were elective courses. Architectural criticism was not even mentioned.

In contrast, substantial progress was made at that time regarding the search for a contemporary Indonesian architectural vocabulary. In 1986, a new campus for the University of Indonesia was completed. The architects who designed the campus were still young at the time, and had just finished their postgraduate studies abroad. Their approach to expressing a contemporary Indonesian architectural identity was based on carrying out thorough studies that aimed at identifying generic types of vernacular Indonesian buildings and then transposing the findings into their designs through an analogy of functions. The new campus became well known and widely popular since the Indonesian president inaugurated it, and it was also featured on television stations throughout the country. At the same time, local governors began insisting that new government buildings in their provinces express a regional identity.

Not surprisingly, such new architecture did not last long because most of the architects assigned to design regionally inspired buildings were neither familiar with the generic types of regional architecture nor with the analogical approach towards architectural design. Instead, they followed an approach that had been prevalent and popular for many years among members of the architectural community in Indonesia, generally referred to as the "formal" design approach. It consisted primarily of placing traditional local roof forms on top of their buildings regardless of differences in scale or of the fact that the new building and the original one from which the forms were borrowed served completely different functions.

The young architects who designed the new campus were also teaching at Indonesian universities. Along with other colleagues of the same generation, they promoted the architecture of Postmodernism to students at leading schools of architecture in the country. By 1989, there was a new generation of young Indonesian architects who had a very different perspective on the architectural discourse of the country, and who also interacted with architectural colleagues of their generation in a different manner than before. Accordingly, they started holding regular meetings among themselves during which they presented their work to an open peer group to generate debate and initiate criticism. This was followed by group visits to notable works of architecture both inside and outside the country. They even nicknamed this activity "architectural pilgrimage" so as to emphasise its importance. Afterwards, they set up what was referred to as the "open house" programme, which provided an open invitation to members of the group, to see recent works of a member of the group and to discuss those works and provide feedback. These young architects also organised exhibitions and published books on their work.

Initially, there were high expectations that such activities would lead to the establishment of a tradition of architectural criticism in the country, but things did not work out that way. These young architects emerged as new idols to students of architecture, and they gradually abandoned their original mission. They soon became the new elites of Indonesian architecture, and were not receptive to criticism from others. They abandoned the tradition of peer group criticism they had initially set up, and the "open house" programme was eventually reduced to no more than a social gathering.

Most architectural magazines in the country went along with this state of affairs because these young architects were trendsetters, and featuring their work increased sales of the magazines. The magazines concentrated on providing beautiful photographs of the architects' works, and made no efforts to provide any deep analysis of them. The development of a tradition of architectural criticism in Indonesia consequently remains an unfulfilled task.

During the 1980s, the leading schools of architecture in Indonesia initiated master's degree programmes. Some of them surprisingly offered specialisations in history and criticism. At that time, there were only six Indonesian architects who had studied the history and theory of architecture abroad as the main subject for their master's or doctoral degrees. A number of architects also did some course work in the history and theory of architecture as part of their graduate studies, while others were convinced that they knew what architectural criticism was all about without the need to take any formal instruction in it. Regardless of this diversity of backgrounds, members of these three groups became core lecturers in these newly established history and theory of architecture specialisations at Indonesian universities.

In assessing these developments, it is important to emphasise that architectural criticism needs to be comprehensive. It needs to consider as many factors responsible for the making of architecture as possible. Accordingly, there must be a clear boundary between the 'history of architecture', which merely deals with technicalities of building production, and 'architectural history', which is the suitable vehicle for architectural criticism. However, it should also be added that such a position may be misleading. If not carried out properly, the instruction of 'architectural history' may end up merely presenting a little bit of information about social, anthropological, psychological, economic and political situations of the period concerned, and providing what is not much more than a compilation of quotes, as well as citing prominent names in related disciplines without adequate elaboration. Numerous problems or questions would be left unanswered. Architectural criticism according to this practice of teaching therefore provides an open-ended debate with no final resolution.

A second stream of criticism depends on rhetoric and on journalistic skills. For this, neither a sound theoretical base nor a methodology is necessary, since it merely relies on having the skill to attract the interest of a wide readership. This is especially the case when the writer tackles governmental policies and the inability of governmental bodies to act properly in particular situations. It does not contain any criticism of individual works. Instead, this stream of writing hails individual architects and their work, since any criticism of architects would not be accepted by the readers, who would condemn the critics as being too personal in their judgements.

A third kind of criticism that has appeared in Indonesia is strongly 'academic' in nature. To some extent, it provides an extension of the critique sessions of design studios at schools of architecture. It combines theories and arguments incorporating history, sometimes with great exaggeration and a lack of methodology. It undoubtedly provides for a boring reading for those outside academic circles, and such publications are therefore limited to specialised journals, papers and university theses; they do not lead to establishing any tradition of architectural criticism. Moreover, architecture students who may have been involved in such writing do not continue it after graduation, but move on to different endeavours.

An attempt was also made to bring architectural criticism into the architectural discourse in Indonesia through seminars on the history and theory of architecture. During the 1980s, three seminars were conducted. The first was a round table meeting that included a limited number of participants. Each participant presented a paper that was supposed to be followed by a thorough discussion. However, the audience members do not seem to have understood what the speakers were presenting, because of their poor theoretical foundations. The second event was a writing competition on architectural theory for which the winners were those who presented the academic style of writing mentioned above. The third event was a seminar where participants presented the abstracts of their master's and doctoral dissertations. Criticism in this event unfortunately was very muted.

It seems that architectural criticism remains a taboo in Indonesia. Being an architectural critic puts one in a rather dangerous position because he or she risks the enmity of many parties. At present, nobody in Indonesia is willing to take such a risk.

[1] Regarding Productivism, see Kenneth Frampton, *Modern Architecture: A Critical History*, rev. and enl. ed., Thames and Hudson, London 1992, pp. 300–305.
[2] See Charles Jencks, *The Language of Post Modern Architecture*, Rizzoli, New York 1977.
[3] See Bruce Allsopp, *A Modern Theory of Architecture*, Routledge and Kegan Paul, London 1977.

VII. CRITICAL CULTURE:
THE ARCHITECTURE OF THE GULF

The Architect as Critic: Reconceiving the Architecture of the Gulf Region

NADER ARDALAN

The critic comes wearing many masks and, as Dennis Sharp has observed, it is necessary to distinguish between them. In this paper, I will address the role of the architect as critic, and illustrate my thoughts by sharing briefly with you three domains, four birth cycles, and one evolving methodology that has been of some value for me.

THREE DOMAINS

The architect, through his practice and the leadership role that he or she must assume as the carrier of the vision of a project, serves as the core and primary commentator on concepts to be perceived, expressed and manifested. His interaction with fellow colleagues in the office, with consultants, with contractors and, most importantly, with his patrons and clients nourishes the primary domain not only of selecting conceptions, but, by critical dialogue, also of eliminating many other conceptions that are not in harmony with the basic vision of a project because of aesthetic, functional, monetary, or philosophic considerations.

The second domain concerns the architect as critic in the field of academia. The regeneration and nurturing of future generations of architects require the critic to be a researcher, teacher and mentor.

The third domain brings the architect fully into the social context by providing opportunities for the contribution of the two previous domains to reach a broad range of society. Here, publications, open lectures and the dissemination of theoretical as well as applied ideas place the architect in the public domain and allow him to influence, albeit tangentially, the direction of society's attitudes and actions towards the built environment.

FOUR BIRTH CYCLES

Psychiatrist Carl Jung elegantly described life's four archetypal stages, and his associate Jolande Jacobi elaborated on Jung's ideas regarding these four stages in her *The Way of Individuation*.[1] According to Jacobi, "metaphorically, we could speak of the most important stations on the way of individuation as four births" (p. 133; fig. 1 here). Also, Thomas Cole painted them in his famous 1842 series entitled *The Voyage of Life*.

Cycle 1: childhood

As a Western-trained architect working in the early 1960s, the basic critical design principles instilled in me were structured around function and technology. These served me well at Skidmore, Owings & Merrill in San Francisco, and later in my first years of architectural practice in Iran, where I dutifully transferred my technological knowledge and used it to convince patrons and fellow colleagues to design and build the first pre-cast, load-bearing concrete towers in Tehran.

Cycle 2: youth

In the early 1970s, I began to research the roots of my own identity through the architectural heritage of Iran, to teach at Tehran University, and to co-author a seminal work entitled *The Sense of Unity*.[2] As an outcome of this research and new consciousness, when commissioned in 1970 to design the Centre for Management Studies in Tehran (established in conjunction with the Harvard Business School), the culture and language of the traditional architecture of Iran became integrated into my primary design thinking. The subsequent publication of the *Habitat Bill of Rights* in 1976 with Josep Luís Sert, Moshe Safdie, Balkrishna Doshi and Georges Candilis further enhanced the value of regionalism in architecture, and allowed me, with my peers, to formulate an international perspective on the qualitative procedures and strategies necessary to the achievement of principles essential to the creation of a wholesome, balanced and equitable habitat.

Suha Özkan later observed that "Ardalan's work was not, however, limited exclusively to the physical aspects of historical form, but encompassed the philosophy and mysticism of Sufi traditions in Iranian Architecture".[3]

This cycle allowed all three domains of the architectural critic to be activated. Professionally, this more culturally sensitive perception of design influenced several colleagues to initiate similar directions of design exploration. Academically, students at Tehran University developed a greater appreciation of their architectural heritage. On the public level, these activities started an architectural trend and provided inspiration for the use of traditional brick technology and space making that received support from the highest patrons of the country.

Cycle 3: maturity

In the late 1970s, there was heightened interest in energy-conscious design due to the increase in world oil prices. It was also during this period that I had the good fortune to have as my consulting associate the great ecologist Ian McHarg, author of *Design with Na-*

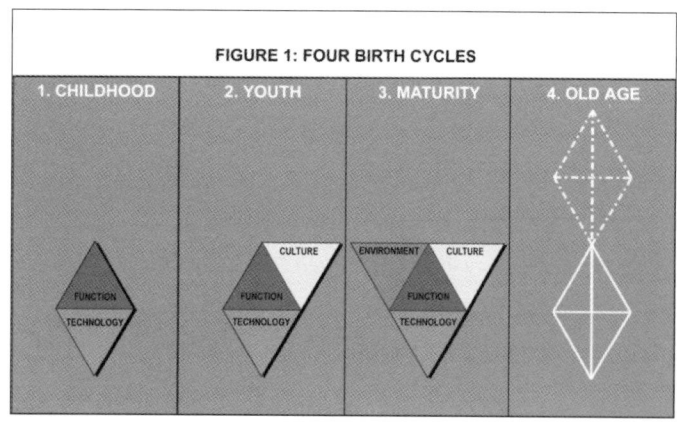

Fig. 1. Four birth cycles.

164

ture.[4] We worked together on a vast environmental park in Tehran named Pardisan, which received a Progressive Architecture Award. We also designed a master plan for a new town for the Petrochemical Company in Mahshahr, Iran.

This environmental consciousness was further enhanced when commissioned to design an inceptional Solar City named Nuran for the Atomic Energy Organisation in Isfahan in 1977. It was at this time that the key four methodological forces of design that have influenced the years to come of my work came together: function, environment, culture and technology.

I explored this methodology academically at Harvard's Graduate School of Design, and socially through my participation in the Steering Committee of the Aga Khan Award for Architecture. The latter broadened the scope of my regional understanding of the Muslim world as it brought us into critical dialogue on how to evaluate and award design concerns stretching from Africa to China, as well as on how to accommodate the spatial needs of Muslims in non-Muslim lands.

This architectural breadth of involvement has characterised the past twenty-five years of my work. During this period, the patronage of outstanding individuals of position, particularly in the Middle East, has allowed the architect as critic to dialogue with professionals, academicians and key decision makers. The results have been as diverse as the clients, but the sustaining perception has been based upon the four design forces mentioned above. Publications in the social domain, such as *The Architectural Review - Middle East* (Spring 1999) and *Architecture+* (July 2002), continue to appear on a regular basis, and the Aga Khan Award has been one of the most faithful couriers of these commentaries on architecture, society and the philosophy of existence.

Cycle 4: wise old man
Having passed the first three stages of Childhood, Youth and Maturity, the fourth cycle offers the challenge, eloquently articulated by Jacobi, "to depart through the door of life and re-enter the vast, unexplored land beyond death, from whence we came".[5] Jung offers the consolation that we will probably never meet a "fully individuated" person, for "the meaning and purpose of life's problem seem to be not in its solution but in our working at it incessantly".[6] Such "incessant work", which has captivated my architectural thinking, began early in my career when I was made aware of the unity within the diversity of cultures, as expressed in the various great architectural traditions of the world. Their universal and common archetypal mythical dimensions (the Platonic *Eidos*) that transcended the limitations of place and time have absorbed my theoretical explorations. Simultaneously, as a practising architect I have also had to appreciate regional and materially limited dimensions (the Platonic *Eidolon*) that have rooted the great architectural traditions to their particular place, climate and symbolism. These have shaped the unique architectural expressions of such traditions and provided their measurable, tangible personalities as well as cultural identities.

Fig. 2. Bird's-eye rendering showing the teaching facilities at the UAE University in al-Ain, United Arab Emirates, KEO International Consultants, 2003.

Two recent projects represent our current thinking at KEO International Consultants, where I am director of design, about the potential of designing with a full consciousness of sustainable design principles based upon the four key design forces.

The first is the Student Centre, School of Architecture, and teaching facilities as well as laboratories at the UAE University in al-Ain. Environmentally adaptive strategies maximise optimum solar and wind orientation by the use of compact forms, an internal student street that connects all parts of the complex, large atria for student gatherings, openings oriented to achieve optimum sun conditions, and the use of light shelves to bounce natural light deep into classrooms. The entire design achieves a very contemporary sense of the traditional Islamic 'sense of place' by having buildings surround and open towards centrally located gardens. Materially, the buildings are clad in a clay tile that harmonises in colour with the natural red hues of the sand dunes surrounding the desert oasis of al-Ain. The project was completed in 2003 and was one of the recipients of the 2004 *Architecture+* awards (fig. 2).

The second project is still in the design phase, but already indicates noticeable innovations in sustainable design strategies. The town centre for Besat New Town in Mahshahr, Iran, is located adjacent to the Jarrahi river. Situated on a thirteen-hectare flat site, the centre includes a retail bazaar, cultural centre, mosque, sports and entertainment complex, business centre, and a great pedestrian esplanade that runs by the river's edge and is polarised around an ontological tower of water. Necessary parking and shaded open space are also provided. The planning of the complex is organic and asymmetric in its fluid geometry, recalling the waves of sand dunes. The forms are compact, and openings are placed towards the north to avoid the direct penetration of the hot sun, and to catch the north-west cooling breezes. The concept of 'mixed mode' technology is applied, enabling natural ventilation during six months of the year through operable windows and *badgirs* (wind towers), thus significantly reducing the need for the use of mechanical air conditioning. It is anticipated that these sustainable techniques and other innovations in building systems will reduce overall energy consumption by thirty per cent. Culturally, the traditional concept of the linear bazaar, so characteristic of Iran, is the organising principle. The sky-lit bazaar is 'green' with trees and flowering shrubs, and a running stream that gets its water from the Jarrahi river flows by natural gravity from north to south and culminates in a spiral fountain before flowing to irrigate further tree lines. Human scale, comfort and pedestrian movement dominate in the harsh environment of this highest radiant energy-gain part of the world. A sustainable microclimate and a spatial order based upon 'positive space systems' can create a working example of how environmentally and culturally relevant design can sustain and celebrate life, even in this extremely climatically stressful context (figs. 3, 4).

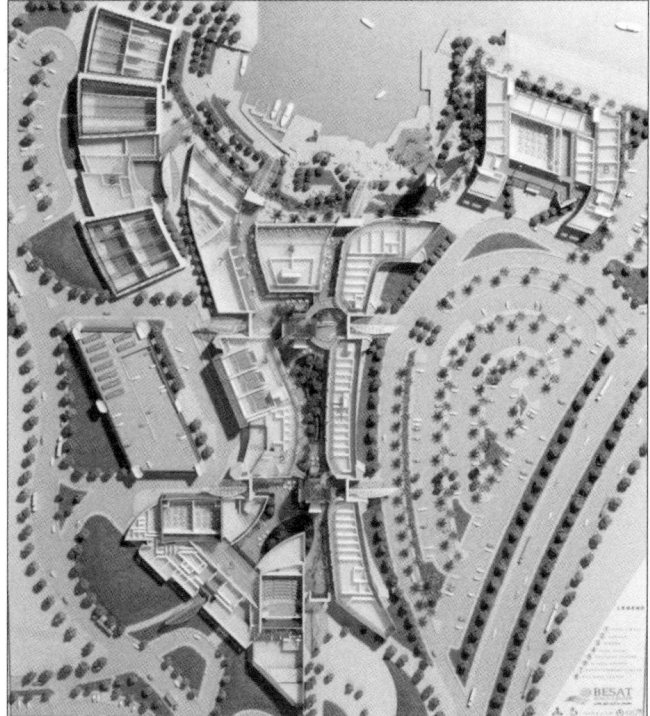

Figs. 3, 4. Design model of Besat Town Centre, Iran, KEO International Consultants (ongoing design project).

The experience of Besat New Town demonstrates another potential example of a contemporary design that is rooted in its context historically, symbolically and environmentally, yet is dynamically new.

How then to design and build in the here and now, while imbuing the 'Work' with the sublime and transcendent dimension, has been the spiritual koan or riddle of my professional life. Having spent the last decade practicing architecture in the regional vortex of the world's primary energy source and the accompanying strife associated with such a place, it has been exceedingly meaningful to have discovered the stillness at the centre of these 'storms' here in Kuwait, from which the potential of great creativity can spring.

Fig. 5. Aerial view of Kuwait City, 1950.

It is interesting to postulate that, as with Carl Jung's four life cycles related to individuals, perhaps cities too exhibit such life cycles. If we use Kuwait City as an example, by 1950 the old town of Kuwait was a mature manifestation of a traditional Arab social system, exhibiting an excellent adaptation, based on necessity, of environmental passive design principles, clustered courtyard housing with clearly differentiated public and private zones, and a sense of cultural identity (fig. 5).

However, by 1970 almost all traces of this traditional fabric and context of life had been demolished, and a new birth cycle had commenced. Naturally, the first cycle was that of Childhood. The imitative forms of Western culture were very much based upon Bauhaus Modernism, which allowed very little room for anything other than function and technology.

In the early 1990s, when I came to Kuwait, just after its liberation, and joined KEO International Consultants, there were the beginnings of a new sentiment in Kuwait that sought cultural identity. One of the first buildings we designed was the Sharq Waterfront Development. We designed a complex inspired by the cultural heritage of the Gulf, together with the functional needs of a contemporary retail-entertainment mall and adaptive technology. This experience resembled very much the second life cycle of Youth, where the city of Kuwait became conscious of its historic roots and national identity.

However, today, as the oil-rich countries of the Gulf region, Kuwait included, are at the threshold of vast new developments due to unique economic conditions, these countries for the most part are regrettably using outdated and unsuitable design models that inevitably will compromise their effectiveness, longevity and historical value.

Although significant advancement in technology and visual design thinking is exhibited by current buildings in Kuwait, proposed or recently built, and although goodwill is intended by the concerned decision makers, the trouble is that the developments and building designs being used are based upon obsolete, energy-consuming prototypes, and suffer from a lack of cultural identity. They seem to have reverted back to the Childhood stage, where function (and also quick economic return), coupled with a dependence on high-energy consumption technologies, pervade the scene. Part of the problem is due to the fact that new sustainable models or prototypes suited and tailored for hot-arid or humid bio-climatic regions that are also culturally relevant have not been fully developed to date. 'Off-the-shelf' Western models with new and dazzling facelifts provide the illusion that the standards of acceptable design have been achieved. Also, the speed of development taking place does not allow designers to give the time needed to develop more suitable design models.

Interestingly enough, our region is not alone in this dilemma. The American Institute of Architects (AIA) recently took a bold step in releasing the following policy statement:

> The AIA recognizes a growing body of evidence that demonstrates current planning, design, construction and real estate practice contribute to patterns of resource consumption that seriously jeopardize the future of the Earth's population [...] We must alter our profession's actions and encourage our clients and the entire design and construction industry to join with us to change the course of the planet's future.[7]

Why is this? What are the underlying causes for this dilemma, and what can be done about it? It must take a paradigm shift of perception both by key decision makers and the public to engender the full dimensions of a new mindset. What will be built in rapid succession over the next five years will burden this society for generations to come.

CONCLUSIONS: IDENTIFYING AN EVOLVING METHODOLOGY
In the next and final phase, the fourth cycle of my own life, I wish to research the preceding cycles, to reflect and act upon the lessons learned from them, and to document possible solutions to key problems observed. Here are a few examples of the problems generally found in the recent architecture of the Gulf and some thoughts on reconceiving the architecture of this region.

1. Sustainable design
Most new buildings that are currently being designed and many that have already been constructed are neither environmentally sustainable nor energy efficient. Few, if any, follow international green building criteria such as those established by the American Leadership in Energy and Environmental Design (LEED™) or the British sustainable design standard BREEAM. Local governments can foster and provide legislation for higher sustainable design standards and provide incentives as well as recognition to those who do produce 'green buildings'. Today, there are cost-effective concepts that can reduce fossil fuel consumption in buildings by fifty per cent, and energy-efficient strategies that can reduce total building power demand significantly. The new paradigm of energy-conscious design can be affordable. It just takes a mindset revolution, a jump into another level of creative thinking and life pattern.

2. Cultural relevance

Few, if any, new buildings show professional sensitivity to either the historical and social patterns, or the cultural symbols of the region. Moreover, new buildings do not address elegantly the transcendent, sublime dimension of universal design considerations. Published studies and demonstrations of culturally relevant principles in schools of architecture and professional societies could develop great awareness of this issue.

3. Politicisation of symbols

The growth of Fundamentalism and the more recent politicisation of traditional signs and symbols have robbed the region of, or inhibited it from, the heritage of its visual language. A re-reading of the history of signs can reintegrate what has been lost or compromised. A deeper study could identify the unity as well as the multiplicity of the visual archetypes of all faiths as a commentary to help dispel the inevitability of the "Clash of Civilisations" mindset that regrettably is now so prevalent in the media.

4. Reformation of linear thinking

As a reformation in philosophic and symbolic thinking to adapt to science and knowledge in the twenty-first century has not been fully experienced in the region, the accepted notion that Islamic architecture must be characterised by the use of symmetry-based Platonic solids and Pythagorean geometry has stilted creative design.

The above few thoughts attempt to address some of the 'traps' that limit creative, innovative and relevant design in the region. Aesthetically and intellectually, these traps tend to make us lose our cultural identity and discourage us from seeing and thinking holistically within the new global consciousness of the "Gaia" principle so well-defined by chemist Sir James Lovelock, which postulates that living matter on our planet functions as a single organism.

Through graphic demonstrations, accompanied and supported by philosophic theory, critical visual dialogue can bring new geometric patterns, orders and forms to the region that can continue to evoke the Islamic tenet of the "Oneness of Existence", but explore the world of fractals and non-linear constructs that reflect the asymmetric structure of the universe being discovered by molecular biology, theoretical physics and astronomy.

The gifted engineer-designer Cecil Balmond states that the "nature of reality is chance and that traditional source of 'order' may only be a small, local, steady state of a much larger random structure". He goes on to demonstrate this observation by reminding us of the example of the different local states and forms of H_2O. Ice transforms to water and then to mist, while all the time two hydrogen and one oxygen atoms are the constant structure and provide the emergent stability, yet are specific in form to the moment of temperature.[8]

Whether ultimate reality is based on chance, destiny, or a dynamic interaction of the two, the symbolic and spiritually sensitive expression of an emergent, energy conscious stability in the art and architecture of the Gulf can be a noble and sustaining vision for future generations.

The website referenced in this essay was accessed in May 2006.

[1] Jolande Jacobi, *The Way of Individuation*, New American Library, New York 1983.
[2] Nader Ardalan and Laleh Bakhtiar, *The Sense of Unity*, University of Chicago Press, Chicago 1973.
[3] Suha Özkan, "Modernity and Tradition: Problem or Potential", in A. Petruccioli and K. K. Pirani (eds.), *Understanding Islamic Architecture*, Routledge Curzon, London and New York 2002, p. 90.
[4] Ian McHarg, *Design with Nature*, Wiley, New York 1995.
[5] Jacobi, *The Way of Individuation* cit., p. 133.

[6] C. G. Jung, Gerhard Adler and R. F. C. Hull, *The Structure and Dynamics of the Psyche (The Collected Works of C. G. Jung)*, vol. 8, Routledge and Kegan Paul, London: Anchor Books, New York 1960, p. 394.
[7] See "High Performance Building Position Statements", in *The American Institute of Architects* (AIA), online. Available at www.aia.org/SiteObjects/files/HPB_position_statements.pdf.
[8] Cecil Balmond (ed.), "Informal", in *Informal*, Prestel, Munich 2002, pp. 115–116.

Desperate Decadence

OLE BOUMAN

Cities arise because of people's basic need to live and work near one another. The city offers freedom, anonymity, possibilities for trade, economies of scale, immediately accessible consumer markets, potentials for employment, in addition to a swarming brew of ideas and innovation that fulfil man's social, psychological and economic needs. The city is an engine of progress.

So it was and so it still seems to be. The growth of the city – the enormous and never-ending expansion of urbanisation – continues to be understood within the context of modernity: people want better lives, and they seek to realise that in the city. To achieve true wealth, you also need to be in the city: in penthouses, high above the dirty streets, but still close to directors' offices, conference rooms, lounge bars, skyboxes, restaurants, and all the other locations imperative to the art of networking. Hence, the city may be understood by its incredible density of people, ideas and interactions.

The city may also be understood through its architecture. We have come to take for granted that those locations with large congregations of works of architecture must be cities. This assumption is the slowly ripened result of a long historical development towards what is conceived as more, higher, freer, better and richer, a solidification of a gradual historical process. And in this process of consolidation, we city dwellers are left to experience the daily hum of car engines or street musicians; the smells of hot dog stands and asphalt; as well as the harsh wind blowing through boulevards or whirling around high rises.

Not quite. The city that exists today is not the end product of a slow process of development, but, at best, one that stands at the beginning of a new and swift one; a city that is not a haphazard creation formed from a coalescence of history, but a simple conception sprung straight from the drafting table. It is not the precipitation of the ambitions of innumerable protagonists, but the execution of one individual or oligarchic decision. The contours of this city are not found in a historic will that took centuries to manifest itself, but in the graphic realisation of a projected image from the here and now. Forget the logo as a symbol of your corporate identity. Gone is the era of the iconic building that has to catch your attention. Now you can simply build an entire skyline as a logo. After the 'Bilbao effect', we now have the 'Dubai effect'. In such a city (even though she lies ringed by a scorching desert), all smells and sounds are banned, even the searing temperatures are made obsolete. They are replaced with commercially acceptable soundscapes, sweet smells and soft breezes. This is the architecture and urbanism of the most evolved form of brand awareness. It looks like a city, but feels like animation. The inhabitants and visitors are not the city's cause, but its legitimacy and profit margin.

That is what you would get if you have the resources necessary for this transformation. So welcome to Dubai, or for that matter to Kuwait City, Doha, Manama, and the other *instant cities* of the oil states. One-dimensionally, they are small dots on the map that have suddenly become rapidly growing ink blots. Two-dimensional silhouettes are literally carved out of the sea, desert and air. Three-dimensionally, completely novel forms of human society have sprung into being. A four-dimensional step is made in the leap from historical origin to ahistoric 'implementation'. Where once, from the *città ideale* to the *ville radieuse*, the complete vision of a city was to remain forever a hallucination, now a full city can be made in a matter of years. You cannot exactly call this the realisation of a dream – it happens too quickly for that. Some allude to this instant city as the most expansive urban event that man has ever known, but this might just be a modern-day form of marketing.

Marketing? Or is there more going on? In general, the Gulf states are described in terms of their extravagance – sometimes also of their decadence. The speed with which complete islands are designed in the sea, the exorbitant cost of construction, the mind-boggling creation of so many square metres, the luxury of the interiors, the overwhelming scale of the airports and high-rise towers, and the most spectacular ski-domes are all expressions of a transgressive drive. Writers from across the publishing spectrum, penning reflective essays to tourist blurbs in in-flight magazines, only use superlatives to describe this new pressure cooker of modernity. Choosing the safe side of the historical battlefield, they limit themselves to anthropologic eulogies that describe yet another phenomenal step forward for mankind.

There is also a rising genre that describes this new step forward in terms of the economic contradiction in capital and social price that these cities require. Here, the social critic has found fertile grounds to express his or her indignation. We now know about the unimaginable exploitation of imported Asian labourers, who for a few dollars a day toil away at creating these dream constructions; and about the Asian women – victims of human trafficking and endemic heartlessness – who work as domestic slaves.

A similar line of reasoning addresses the noteworthy relationship between these hyper-modern societies and their roots in tribal and Islamic cultures. Diverse authors ask themselves how it is possible that these regions of decadence have escaped the large-scale terrorist attacks that the West has come to fear. Has Dubai not earned, by the Wahhabi yardstick, more of God's wrath than any other city?

173

Then of course, there is the ecological perspective. This focuses on the threat to nature that is the natural consequence of unbridled construction. The constantly resurfacing example of this is the possible deformation of coast lines along the Arabian-Persian Gulf as a result of the reckless construction of several artificial islands along the coast. This is dismaying news even before one considers these cities' flagrant waste, not only of natural resources, but also of a seemingly limitless stream of money. From this perspective, Dubai and the "Do Buys" around it may be the last big kick to which mankind can treat itself. An enormous potlatch, based on the riches of crude oil accumulated over millions of years.

What is striking in these interpretations is that they are attempts to describe the developments of the Gulf region within familiar and known theoretical frameworks. But is it possible that this is an emerging world for which we as yet have no concepts? Or maybe this is a world that has grown beyond theoretical constructs? Could this be a world that is determined, regardless of consequence, to establish itself beyond sense and reason? Shouldn't every attempt at understanding fail when confronted with the naked truth? Isn't the rising world along the western coast of the Gulf better understood as an unconscious experiment in Social Darwinism, disguised as paradise?

The experiment has multiple dimensions. First, there is an unprecedented degree of waste. Moderation is nowhere to be found. The investments that are necessary for these urban conurbations, amusement parks, airports and offshore engineering feats are financed mainly by oil profits. Anyone trying to imagine what kind of wealth is necessary for this will find no historical precedents to aid them. The astronomical profits earned from high oil prices will only continue to rise in response to increasing demand. So much capital is now available that it has begun to exceed human imagination; that is, if it comes to imagining what can be done with it. This flood of resources (next to capital, there also seems to be endless space and building material) has killed any lingering acknowledgment of scarcity. Prudence and caution have disappeared. Money, which will never have the same profit margin as the product by which it was originally earned, must be spent. You can ask yourself if it is even possible to speak of 'investments'.

The experiment has moral implications when one examines the individuals making these projects possible. The Gulf region is, without precedent, home to the widest disparities between rich and poor that exist in the world. Even for those who would believe that these labourers earn an adequate salary, and even if such salaries actually are being paid to these labourers, one can see that when comparing these salaries to the sums of money available in those countries, one can only speak of a modern form of slavery. A flood of capital also implies an endless source of labour. It is questionable, however, if this situation can be judged by the parameters of social theory. Indeed, despite the abominable circumstances to which these labourers are subjected, is it not all based on free will after all? Open coercion on a large scale is not verifiable. Perhaps there should be an exploration of what 'free will' actually entails in these regions.

A third dimension of the experiment is the degree of coincidence. The prosperity of many of the citizens of Dubai, Kuwait, or Qatar has little to do with their intrinsic value, their personal productivity, or talent. The realisation of a world valued at the level of a seven-star hotel is not a well-earned reward for hard labour, but has everything to do with the coincidental fact that oil exists underground. This is particularly ironic for a nomadic society, which lived for centuries in temporary settlements, and now has every interest in creating cities close to oil wells, with the demarcation of territories and the forging of alliances with the global powers that can assure that this wealth will remain in the same hands.

Perhaps it is a deep understanding of the coincidence of wealth that prompted the fortuity of forms in which this world has been moulded. It is clear that a world can be created in which forms do not rest on a canon of legitimised styles, but on the capricious tendencies of the market and whims of the client. This results in a city landscape that can formally be described as arbitrary. The very search for excess and the need to make an impression has led to the mass production of 'genius'.

But the waste, the inequality and the coincidence become even more penetrating when we understand how this artificial world is the eye in a hurricane of natural disaster and warfare. In an oasis surrounded by the battles for Kashmir, earthquake rubble in Pakistan, the confrontation politics of Iran, the civil war in Iraq, the Israeli-Palestinian conflict, the genocide and famines of East Africa, and the chilling destruction of the tsunami, Muslims, Jews, Christians, Buddhists and especially agnostics come together to celebrate the epitome of human wealth. If one thing is obvious, it is that this celebration is oblivious to the encroaching misfortune and disaster.

Perhaps this is the most experimental aspect of this whole development: that desperate optimism has created its own playground, virtually blind to the world around it. It is decadence as total denial of truth; but also decadence as the only hope in creating something so terribly magical that it might survive the age of oil.

The City in Hiding: Response to Ole Bouman's "Desperate Decadence"

SALLY KHANAFER, AFNAN AL RABAIAN AND AYESHA AL SAGER

Born and raised in the Gulf region, we tend to look at the subject Mr Bouman discussed in his article in a different light. We are more aware of, and sensitive to, the subtitles, differences and changes that occur between the different cities that make up the Gulf. We are more conscious of the process of events and patterns that resulted in the cities of the Gulf that his essay "Desperate Decadence" describes. The 'Dubai effect' was used as a metaphor to describe the different cities of the region. To us, the 'Dubai effect' exists, but not in the manner the essay described it. The 'Dubai effect' is a metaphor for the accelerated boom these different cities are undergoing, perhaps even more aggressively now than ever before. However, it does not allow us to gain further insight into these individual cities.

A great divide exists within our cities. It is important to note that the cities in which we *dwell* do not follow the common typology of a city. This divide separates the city in half. In one half lies the *dream* city: a *shell* devoid of social, cultural and psychological needs; a shell that serves the creation of a purely materialistic capital. In the other half lies the *human* space: a *city* that is based on *people* and on their daily needs and interactions. It is here that we find our *moments*: kids playing football, men walking to the mosque, people making their daily grocery rounds, women gathering for tea at midday, and so on. It is here that we find charity organisations, daycare centres, schools, big houses, small houses, everything that makes every neighbourhood – or mini city – complete.

This leads us to examine the process through which the *divided city* was established. The origins of these cities date back to over four hundred years. Settlers and nomads moved into previously uninhabited areas to build cities that fulfilled and symbolised all their needs. Over time, these cities expanded – in the manner that any normal city would –, creating tightly woven urban fabrics. Four centuries later, with the discovery of oil, sudden changes occurred. The base on which these cities survived was suddenly shattered. New needs, new necessities and new aspirations emerged. A new set of solutions that are responsive to these newfound needs had to be formulated. By the 1960s, mass-produced concrete buildings became the brush that painted the city. With time, commerce mainly dictated the evolution of the city, and consequently created a city whose concern was not that of its inhabitants, but that of its profit. It was the driving force in the creation of the shell. The divide thus began to appear. The inhabitants, however, continued to dwell outside the shell, within the values of the original city.

The effect of the divide is evident in people's daily lives. This effect exists in various degrees in the different cities of the Gulf. For example, within Kuwait City, this divide is obvious in every aspect: psychologically, socially, physically, and of course architecturally, where the separation between human space and the dream city is clearly manifested; that is, the architecture in the human space is totally different from that in the dream city. In Manama, the divide is somewhat more blurred; the separation is not as apparent as in Kuwait because the dream city and human space join together and merge at certain points. In Dubai, the divide does not seem apparent. Does human space exist in these cities? Or is it too weak to even be noticeable? Upon closer inspection, human spaces actually do begin to surface in small pockets. They, however, are so small in scale that the shell – the projected image of the city – completely overshadows them.

Using the analogy of the in-flight magazine, whose blurbs are usually trivial, expresses the way in which the cities of the Gulf are generally looked upon. Dubai is represented by a palm tree tattooed in the middle of the sea. Yet, is this really the image of the city? This is as absurd as suggesting that the Statue of Liberty is the image of the city of New York. So where then is the city?

The city is the human space hidden behind the shell. The shell then is no more than a mask we choose to wear. By wearing it, we are seen as being 'oblivious' to the world around us. It makes us look as if we are reliving a new age of 'decadence'. However, it is the world that put us on a course that led us to wear a mask. The waves of globalisation came in full force and have engulfed us. To adapt to a world that is constantly changing beneath our feet, we created a dream city, a shell. This shell distorts the human space behind it. A city then no longer may be judged by its postcard imagery.

With special thanks to Ali Al-Khaled.

Criticism and the Gulf: A Vision for the Future

PETER DAVEY

One of the most interesting contrasts emerging from the Kuwait seminar was the difference between well-meaning liberal critics (mostly from the West), who were keen to promote concepts such as regionalism, environmental consciousness and the importance of *genius loci*, and people from countries that take their models from what is actually built in the West, rather than what critics say should be built. Darab Diba, editor of *Memari va Shahrsazi* (Architecture and Urbanism) in Tehran, explained that young Iranians do not want to "talk about notions of identity; they do not want to discuss tradition and history. They want Modernity: a wider platform with richer diversity. The models are in the West." Yet both Timur Turekulov, editor of *Kumbez* in Kazakhstan, and Dina Sattarova, editor of *Dizain i Novaia Arhitectura* (Design and New Architecture) from Tatarstan in the Russian Federation, argued for the importance of a regionalism based on tradition in attempting to resist globalisation and Russification.

Globalisation, at its most disastrous, dominated the view through the shaded windows of the room in which the group's meetings were held. Like the other prosperous cities of the Gulf, Kuwait is visually and urbanistically dominated by powerful but sadly outdated models based on the Post-modernist (PoMo) prototypes that were popular in the West in the last decades of the twentieth century. PoMo was never more than a movement devoted to formal expression. At its best, it was concerned with generating a sense of urbanity in contrast to the grey, utilitarian, amorphous cityscapes of late Modernism. At their worst, PoMo architects competed with each other to make the most outrageous and dominating object buildings, divorced from context, history, or anything but the expression of wealth and power.

It is this kind of PoMo that dominates the Gulf in cities carved up into sterile urban islands by multi-lane motorways (in Kuwait these are not as destructive as the ones in Dubai, but more are promised). An exhibition by the Kuwait Society of Engineers that took place at the same time as this seminar showed that this tendency is likely to continue, with slightly different models. The most obviously wilful and extravagantly formalist Western projects are chosen and multiplied. Many more towers are to be expected: twisted, writhing, plain, or coloured, bulging in unexpected places. In an architectural culture that always seems ready to seize on the second-rate and destructive of urbanity, blobs will surround the bases of some of them like greasy scum round tortured sticks in a polluted pond.

All this is made the more tragic because, as Nader Ardalan pointed out, the Gulf could be a crucible from which new environmentally aware architecture and urbanism might be forged. With huge amounts of ambient energy pouring down from the sky, and enjoying great terrestrial riches, the area could become a wonderfully inventive testing ground for architecture and city planning, instead of being a frenetic exposition of the second-hand and second-rate. Jassim Qabazard, deputy chairman of the Kuwait Society of Engineers, explained that the professional climate is changing, and that forms of architecture capable of responding to the great bounty of the sun are beginning to emerge, but there are few signs of them yet.

One of the most surprising aspects of the conference was the lack of criticism by the assembled critics of their surroundings. This undoubtedly was caused partly by a reluctance to criticise our co-hosts, the Kuwait Society of Engineers. All of us found it difficult to be adversely critical, but for some, it was worse than for others. Mashary Al-Naim, an editor of the Saudi Arabian *Albenaa* (Building), pointed out that there is no criticism in Arab culture, or in the Muslim world in general, because critical remarks are considered impolite. And, as there is little or no democracy, there are only a few expressions of opinion in public. For instance, planning cannot be criticised because it is a manifestation of government policy.

Ingeborg Flagge, until recently director of the Deutsches Architektur Museum in Frankfurt, seized on such paradoxes of architectural criticism. She believed that most architectural criticism is worthless – almost always public relations for iconic buildings by well-known architects. There is surely much sense in her position. Magazines compete with each other to have first coverage of buildings by super-star architects. Critics rarely attack any aspect of the work of such architects, partly – it must be admitted – out of politeness, but also out of self-interest.

Criticism is not conducted in a vacuum. All publications emerge from a business structure; they must make a profit (or receive subsidies) to survive, so the nature of the business is immensely influential on its products. For instance, perhaps the most fundamental reason why there can be no adverse criticism of local buildings in the magazines of the Gulf area is that they depend on income from local advertising, which would be withdrawn in the face of critical attack. All magazine editors are aware of such pressures, even if they are applied lightly. When I was editor of *The Architectural Review*, although there was no clearly articulated policy, I was very well aware that the firm's businessmen would be very distressed and angry if I published too many (for them) articles on housing in developing countries because such articles would attract no advertising.

In fact, there are almost no platforms for discussion of such issues. Omar Akbar, director of the Bauhaus Foundation in Dessau, castigated architects and their critical cronies for ignoring the hundreds of millions of people who live in the slums of the world. A rather unfair comment, perhaps, at a seminar run by the Aga Khan Award for Architecture, which is virtually the only organisation that has consistently explored and celebrated excellence in designing for the poor. But, as others have pointed out, in developing countries, architecture is regarded as elitist and therefore of little consequence.

A further problem is perhaps caused by the fact that in the Middle East architecture and civil engineering are virtually amalgamated, with the engineers tending to dominate professional organisations. This clearly has the effect of marginalising architects into making meaningless formal gestures, while encouraging engineers to think in the old-fashioned way about how to solve individual aspects of design (for example, internal temperature control) without relating them to the whole.

The Gulf offers amazing opportunities for generating new architectures that will be sustainable for the planet and for both rich and poor (large numbers of whom live there as expatriate workers). The means are all there, and parts of the seminar give hope that the will may be emerging too.

Critical Culture:
Lifting the Fog on Kuwait City

YASMIN SHARIFF

We shape our buildings; thereafter they shape us, Winston Churchill

We are in a cultural fog – the equivalent of a sand storm in the desert. A storm generated by the movement of labour and resources that is unparalleled in the history of mankind. Urban areas are rapidly expanding and the virtual world is shrinking. News of the fog has immediate and serious political, economic, environmental and social consequences, both locally and globally.

Forces of globalisation have created an international culture where the experience of the modern city, be it Manhattan, Munich, or Mumbai, has strong similarities. They have the same shops, the same glass towers and satellite dishes silhouetting the skyline, and the same hamburger joints punctuating blocks of development. There are Chinatowns in Los Angeles and London, and Indian corner shops in Bradford and Barcelona. Buildings designed in London by people from all over the world are being detailed in countries as far away as Vietnam, and built for a mixed population by foreign workers (often Eastern European). The sense of space and the cultural identity rooted in a particular place for an indigenous group of people are rapidly being eroded, and the experience of cities is becoming much more homogeneous. It is not surprising that we are in a cultural fog and in shifting sands that obscure who and where we are.

Place-making has become increasingly complex at a time when anything is possible. Growing a design that responds to the special nature of the site and its history, the client and the community is a difficult and risky business without any guarantees of success, or, indeed, what it will look like. It is much easier to pluck a scheme from the 'international database' and park it on the allocated lot. Facsimile developments are being passed off as the real thing.

When asked about what a city should be like, the renowned city commentator and urbanist Jane Jacobs responded:

> It should be like itself. Every city has differences, from its history, from its site, and so on. These are important. One of the most dismal things is when you go to a city and it's like 12 others you've seen. That's not interesting, and it's not really truthful.[1]

In his book *The Rise of the Creative Class*, American economist Richard Florida highlights that "quality of place" is an essential factor for a successful community. Florida emphasises that replacing the old and authentic with new and generic facsimiles of neighbourhoods or retail districts is proving to be unsuccessful.[2]

Some of the basic lessons to be learnt from the work of Jacobs and Florida are the significance of cultural infrastructure – an essential ingredient for successful place-making. Human beings are social animals. We cannot survive without social interaction; and cultural infrastructure facilitates, or even engineers, this interaction. Cities with poor cultural infrastructure are like houses without 'living rooms', that is, prisoners of functionality. Business districts filled with skyscrapers and security guards are hostile territory to anyone who strays off the street. There is little fertile ground for a free exchange of ideas, and the few places where this exchange is possible have prospered, for example cafés and shopping malls.

In the case of Kuwait City, the venue for this seminar, a most dynamic and interesting place where people can meet informally is al-Sharq Shopping Mall located on the outskirts of the city (see pls. 38–40). Al-Sharq Waterfront mixed use development has a distinctive 'Arabian' silhouette with forms derived from wind towers. The project tackles many difficult social, cultural and environmental issues. The social value of this project is greatly underrated despite the fact that it is one of the main venues for Kuwaitis to meet in an informal way. The market spaces capture the sounds, smells and excitement of a traditional souk, and modern requirements are integrated into the scheme in a sensitive and stimulating manner. The internal atrium spine provides valuable spaces for people to interact. The shops, restaurants and cinemas have become attraction points that invite people to come out of their homes and have a day out. In effect, this shopping mall is a mini-city that provides the experience of the old souk. The challenge for Kuwait City lies in using the lessons learnt from this and other developments to transform and inform urban design on a much larger scale. Kuwait City is in danger of gaining a collection of very expensive skyscrapers that may be successful in their own right, but are not integrated into the lifeblood of the city. Each skyscraper is like a room in a house without a living room.

People crave stimulation, not escape. The failure of many city centres may be directly linked to zoning laws that isolate retail, office and industrial development, and that regard the developed suburban model as an ideal. Suburbia has kept people away from city centres and has encouraged out-of-town living in developments that have poor cultural infrastructure. Suburbia was designed to provide an escape from the polluted and congested city. It isolates and fragments communities since it lacks social spaces where diverse groups of people can interact. To build a community that can survive and prosper in this rapidly evolving age requires higher levels of quality of place than suburban models can provide. By its very nature, suburbia is low-density and it disperses people. Successful places, as Florida describes, teem with people interacting in formal and informal ways, with a blend of cafés, sidewalk musicians, small galleries and bistros, where it is hard to draw the line between performers and spectators. Here people can pack their time full of dense, high-quality, multidimensional experiences. The model of the medieval city, compact and dynamic, with industries relocated and streets cleaned up, is once more an attractive option.

Cultural infrastructure can be injected into existing areas to enliven them. This, in fact, needs to be an essential part of new developments. Libraries, media centres, galleries, museums, cafés, and so on, are the living rooms of urban life. In these public places, the community can nurture a sense of pride and belonging not only locally but also globally. The Spanish city of Bilbao could not have been propelled onto the world stage only by policies to clean it up and sort out its physical infrastructure. This dying city has been jump-started onto the world stage by its cultural infrastructure: the street life, music, dance, as well as the "Guggy". This term of endearment for the 1997 Guggenheim Museum that Frank Gehry designed for the city is itself an indicator of the sense of pride and belonging that people feel for this development.

In his Scully Seminar Speech, delivered on the occasion of receiving the National Building Museum's (Washington, DC) 2005 Vincent Scully Prize, Prince Karim Aga Khan succinctly summed up the challenge we face:

> I believe profoundly that architecture is not just about building. It is a means of improving people's quality of life. At its best, it should mirror the plurality of cultural traditions and the diverse needs of communities, both urban and rural. At the same time it must employ modern technologies to help fulfill desirable aspirations for the future.[3]

Lifting the 'fog' on Kuwait City is a complex and difficult process. Holding this seminar in Kuwait City is a significant first step in taking stock of a critical intervention that starts to inform about how to maximise the human, social and economic capital of this city. Clues of the city's distinctiveness are apparent and could provide anchors for developing its cultural infrastructure. Islamic civilisation has grown out of the desert. It shows a mastery of garden design, water engineering, and energy-efficient and passive energy systems that are still relevant today. The desert climate demands a different approach to urban planning than a downtown Miami model. Grass verges may be replaced by native species or desert plants that need little artificial watering. Skyscrapers competing for attention on the skyline may be linked by an expansion of the souk network and by providing a socially stimulating and energy-efficient passage through the city with innovative transport suited to the short 'long distances'. Institutions as diverse as the Centre for Diabetic Research and Treatment, the al-Babtain Central Library for Arabic Poetry and the Tareq Rajab Museum could break out of their confines and infiltrate the shopping malls and streets of the city.

At first sight, it seems as though there is little history in Kuwait City. The peoples of this land were nomadic and it is not surprising that not much has been built in ancient times. New developments do not have to rely solely on physical culture for their sources of inspiration. There seems little to use as a historic anchor, yet Kuwait is at the doorstep of ancient trade routes connecting India to Europe and East Africa. There are routes leading directly to the holy cities of Mecca and Medina, and picturesque dhows sail into the docks. The sounds and smells of this port area have strong connections with Zanzibar and Broach, Yemen and Juba, and evoke tales from the Arabian Nights, Sinbad and the Queen of Sheba.

Dynamic cities have active communities that are able to use the city as a stage to host events. The American city of Phoenix, Arizona, may have its art walks, but perhaps Kuwaiti streets could compete with their poetic chants or rhythmic drumming. Culture is not a static historic entity; it is constantly changing and dynamic. What is important is to nurture creative talent and to maximise human capital by capturing people's imagination and inventiveness, and by facilitating their participation in civil society.

The challenge for architects, developers and city authorities is to capture the essence of the place and not mimic the past or foreign exotica. There is a need to recognise the critical role of culture and to make it an integral part of the urban infrastructure. Without serious consideration of cultural infrastructure, cities are nothing but a collection of soulless buildings vying with each other for the latest architectural styles and fads, vulnerable to extinction when fashions change and people leave because they crave something more genuine and dynamic.

Cultural infrastructure is not merely about designing mixed-use urban areas with cafés, theatres and boulevards. Physical spaces are stage sets, props that are useless without engagement and dynamic participation. There is no single solution – a one size fits all; each area will have its own distinctive assets. Nothing is set in stone. The shifting sands of time are forever with us.[4]

All the websites referenced in this essay were accessed in May 2006.

[1] Jane Jacobs, interviewed by Bill Steigerwald, "City Views: Urban Studies Legend Jane Jacobs on Gentrification, the New Urbanism, and Her Legacy", in *Reason*, online, June 2001. Available at www.reason.com/0106/fe.bs.city.shtml. Regarding Jacobs' ideas, see Jane Jacobs, *Dark Age Ahead*, Random House, New York 2004, and *The Death and Life of Great American Cities*, Random House, New York 1961: Vintage Books, New York and Toronto 1992.

[2] Richard Florida, *The Rise of the Creative Class: And How It Is Transforming Work, Leisure, Community and Everyday Life*, Basic Books, New York 2004. See also Richard Florida, "The Rise of the Creative Class", in *Washington Monthly*, online,

May 2002. Available at www.washingtonmonthly.com/features/2001/0205.florida.html#byline.

[3] For the full text of the speech, see www.akdn.org/speeches/2005Jan26.htm.

[4] For insightful theories and ideas relating to the making of successful cities, see Iain Begg (ed.), *Urban Competitiveness: Policies for Dynamic Cities*, The Policy Press, Bristol 2002; Malcolm Gladwell, *The Tipping Point: How Little Things Can Make a Big Difference*, Little, Brown and Company, New York 2000; and Richard Sennett, *The Culture of New Capitalism*, Yale University Press, New Haven 2006.

VIII. BRINGING IT TOGETHER

Notes on a Seminar Session

ROBERT IVY

What is the nature of architectural criticism today? As we write these recapitulations of our meeting in Kuwait, the field is changing, supercharged by energies unleashed by electronic media. Daily and weekly news sources are withering, leaving the formerly authoritative positions of our chief critics wavering in an ambiguous netherworld. The democratisation of information brought on by the World Wide Web concurrently decimates established hierarchies of taste, leaving us all to debate just what role, and what position, the critic will occupy in contemporary culture, as mediator between objective fact, experience, and human cognition and emotion. Are critics necessary, and, if so, for whom? Such was the setting for the second session of this seminar on architectural journalism and criticism.

The architect Hani Rashid, who inaugurated this second session with introductory remarks entitled "The Nature of Architectural Criticism", issued a declaration of ubiquitous change. Citing the "fluid existence" of contemporary life, in which global citizens move freely and find interpersonal connections through digital means, he outlined a new, vaguely troubling view of criticism today. A primary question he raised concerning the audiences for criticism seems central to his subsequent argument. For in outlining a litany of criticism's limitations, the germane issue seems to be the people for whom such radically differing forms of criticism are aimed – audiences that vary, and publications that vary in response.

Rashid outlined the intended audiences, beginning with the mainstream popular news media, including *El Pais*, *The Guardian*, and *The New York Times*, and citing the dichotomy between coverage of the global and the local. He asked rhetorically whether such newspaper coverage is not inevitably coloured by its place of origin (and thereby limited in its concerns about larger matters). Trade journals, by contrast, such as *L'Architecture d'Aujourd'hui*, *Memar* and *A+U*, while intended for professional architects, might find other readers engaged in design and construction, including constructors, owners and other design professionals. At their best, the journals 'reach beyond' themselves, including academic arguments and theoretical ideas within their pages.

He cited the "problematic" but influential pop publications that reach a mass audience of (mainly younger) readers enamoured of the design culture. While their treatment tends towards the "superficial", they are spreading knowledge and appreciation of architecture and design to a broad, educated audience. In contrast, academic journals "focused on the fielding of ideas and criticism" appeal only to a rarified few. Weaving throughout Rashid's arguments was the Internet, replete with blogs and unsolicited commentary, which he likened to a "tidal wave". Without belabouring the point, Rashid asked, given the variety of audiences for contemporary criticism and commentary, and the expansion of the media, are we "the blind leading the blind?"

Kamran Afshar Naderi, architectural critic with the Iranian publication *Memar*, suggested that criticism be grounded in a methodology or approach. Criticism, rather than free-form expressionism, can inform the development of future architecture, elevating the field's importance. Seen from this perspective, decisions about the presentation of architecture take on critical aspects: in photographing a building, he stated, the "relevant aspects" need to be addressed. Architecture assumes importance within its culture, its environment, or economy, and worthwhile criticism can serve an educational role, instructing others into its values.

Afshar Naderi proposed that criticism can help others, including clients, think about architecture in different ways. The critical perspective, both interpretive and judicial, can be of particular value when clear criteria are present within the argument. Such acts of judgement need not be what the architect had in mind during the design or implementation; instead, the critic can apply filters as diverse as history, environmental concerns, societal or personal human needs, and context. By stating the criteria, the critic can differentiate between the architecture of experimentation or purely formal invention and architecture that "can be disseminated in society". Criticism, in Naderi's view, transcends "fault-finding", consisting rather of a search for architecture's values in its relativistic universe.

Frames of reference, similar in intent to the previous critic, dominated the discussion of Ali Cengizkan. He cited the need for an inclusive palette of considerations, including social, aesthetic, historic and economic, as did Kamran Afshar Naderi. Cengizkan also called for the appreciation and awareness of the audiences served by criticism, which might include public opinion, professionals, administrators, users, customers and citizens. He called for critics to heighten the awareness of others to contemporary architecture's "meta-narratives", the overarching messages and ideological positions that characterise today's designs.

Critics invariably promote Modernism, Cengizkan posited, sometimes to the detriment of the communities they serve. The issues that surround architectural projects, however, tend towards complexity, not a narrow range of stylistic choice, which too much criticism provides. Today's writers should be "highly critical of every contemporary phenomenon", he suggested. As an example, he referred to a case study – the Dubai Towers in Istanbul. These extremely expensive, ultra-tall (300-metre) additions to the Istanbul skyline, while seductive at a certain level, would bring challenges to Istanbul's urban infrastructure and add to already present crowding. Urban questions, rather than merely stylistic ones, should have concerned critical discourse surrounding them.

Luis Fernández-Galiano took the contrarian approach. "Critics don't lead architects," he said, "and architects don't lead the world." In Fernández-Galiano's world view, the ethics of architecture take second place. He asserted that "despotic" regimes often actually produce great architecture, while "free societies rarely produce good architecture". The critic issued a call for the colloquium to take a moment of self-assessment, and then realise that critics are at their core writers. As such, they lack central authority, but instead command feelings that may tend towards the odd or the morbid. Certainly they are marginalised.

Fernández-Galiano stated that critical writers maintain a "very visual attitude" towards the world. Their culture is a shared one, including similar personal profiles, similar language, history and heroes. This private language, intended for an intelligent audience, must not be cultivated for the media, but for the intended recipients. Architects, while achieving greater fame, nevertheless are powerless. "We must be allowed to have our obsessions," he stated. "Architectural criticism is elegiac."

Louise Noelle Gras followed up Fernández-Galiano's arguments by restating the individuality and centrality of the critic herself or himself. It may be possible to categorise works of art and architecture as ideas, and to subject them to rigorous study, but final critical judgement "cannot be totally objective," she said. Much depends on the individual consciousness of the critic, exercising her or his own consciousness and experiences on the objects in question, as well as the social milieu surrounding the critic – her or his peers and the public.

She mentioned, as did most, the extraordinary range of possible subjects that surround most architecture, including its possible urbanism or placement, but also its finer-grained aspects, including interior design, special structure, active systems and lighting. She did not shy away from questions about the personal aspects of the makers, when their study adds to a germane argument. Ultimately, judgement, residing within the critic, must inform the choices of subject matter.

Noelle argued for strong arguments whenever critics approach a mass audience, which allows the public to identify with the message. Theory has efficacy in reaching people by constructing arguments that are apprehensible and lending "supporting voices". Ultimately, the critic's position is invaluable to architecture, since architects themselves may understand their work and its motivation, but lack words to express themselves. Architects may see; others read.

Panellists subsequently briefly discussed questions of criticism among themselves. Jose Lluis Hortet, Suneet Paul, Jean-Michel Place and Renata Holod acted as respondents. Hortet underscored the importance of the global perspective, particularly as it intersects with urbanism. Paul differentiated between architectural journalism and architectural criticism, each of which exists at a different level of understanding. Place spoke as a publisher devoted to magazine publishing, while reiterating architecture's role in upholding "planetary values". Holod considers critics as "public intellectuals" who maintain a private language that can recognise "dissonance" in the presence of inept or inappropriate architecture.

A central fact left unaddressed within this otherwise lively discussion lies in the explosion of information and its implications on the critical position. Newspapers are changing, perhaps inalterably, but magazines continue to proliferate. While Rashid and others touched on magazines, for example, they failed to mention that in the United States alone, there are currently some 6,600 magazines in publication, and the number is growing. Web sites present an incalculable expansion, and many of them are devoted to design. Even publications like *Business Week* now feature an architecture component within their virtual versus their printed pages.

How then to parse through such an expanding universe? The credible critic, whether grounded in experience, intuition, or language, can play an expanding role, serving as a cosmic Virgil to the wanderer through the inferno and purgatory that comprises today's universe of information. There seems to be a place for the trusted voice as well as for the untested masses, who well up unannounced and state their positions. As critic after critic attested (with the provocative counter-argument of Luis Fernández-Galiano), however, a continual awareness of audience and milieu remain central to the critic's relevance to architectural discourse.

This essay and the quotations included in it are based on the presentations delivered at the seminar rather than on the final essays documented in this monograph.

Epilogue: Everybody's a Critic

MICHAEL SORKIN

There is an ad on American TV – for a home alarm system – that depicts a comical burglar in a striped prison uniform sitting behind bars as he is interviewed by an off-screen voice. The burglar describes the overgrown lawn – a 'sure sign' – that led him to conclude the inhabitants were away and attempt a break-in. But, asks the interviewer, didn't you see the obvious medallion of the home security company? The embarrassed burglar responds in high annoyance: "Jeez! Everybody's a critic!"

For architecture, everybody actually is. We are always in and around architecture and cannot escape its influence – coercive, delightful, useful, or compromising – and it has always been so. It is part of what marks us as a species, something that – like the highly developed use of tools – is intrinsic to our identity. The press has just announced an effort to unravel the Neanderthal genome, which will surely affirm that we humans share most of our genetic character with this ancestor (much as we do with chimps and nematodes and our other carbon-based cousins). This activity of tracing back also seems an irresistible aspect of our difference, encoded in the structure of our curiosity, whether we account for it via our innumerable theisms, or more scientifically through the search for the evolutionary alpha-point, the moment when some primordial slime was energised and realigned to become 'life'.

Architecture too is built up from its origin tales, the taxonomy of its lineages, always argued backward from some privileged present. We insist on beginnings, on being little gods who labour to create our universes (and then take a break). The famous primitive hut, the first habitation, establishes the myth of architecture's rationality: the idea that shelter was, for us, something motivated by experience, not simply doing 'what comes naturally'. We do not imagine a conference of swallows or beavers from which descended – via their analysis of the mode of production of foodstuffs, the family, protection from predation and inclemency, the need to live in exclusive communities, or even from a spontaneous moment of conviviality – the idea of the nest or the dam. We, on the other hand, demand such a moment to establish the idea of our agency and our capacity for transformation. It seems teleologically impossible to simply think that we were always already sheltering animals.

The same patterns of filiation dominate and defend the way we do our critical business. If we look – as others in this publication have – to writers on architecture and the visual world, including Marcus Vitruvius Pollio from the first century BC; Johann Joachim Winckelmann, Marc-Antoine Laugier, Immanuel Kant, and Georg Wilhelm Friedrich Hegel from the eighteenth and early nineteenth centuries; John Ruskin and William Morris from the nineteenth century, as well as Heinrich Wölfflin, Ernesto Rogers, Bruno Zevi, Gilles Deleuze, and Jacques Derrida from the twentieth, it is all remarkably patrimonial: a tribal anxiety about influence. Indeed – unlike Vitruvius, whose fantasies were for the *hut* – we nowadays seek to understand and (if we can) to justify our ways with less reference to the object of our gaze than to the techniques of our own observation, fixated on our telescopes but losing sight of the stars. This relentless narrowing to a bellelettristic or academic paradigm – the paradigm of writing – has served both to distance us from architecture itself – by inventing it too narrowly – and from its primal scenes: the interaction of space and habitation.

A distinguished psychoanalyst once usefully observed that you do not need to be an architect to hit your head against the wall. Nor, one might add, to be a critic in order to shout "ouch!" This publication is full of lamentations: as critics, we gather to collectively bemoan our meagre reach and to produce ourselves as victims of animus or (worse!) indifference. From the West, we hear about the baleful impact of big money, the superficiality of 'starchitecture', the corruptions of hyper-consumption, and the sheer philistinism of it all. From the East, we hear about confrontations of tradition and modernity, old-fashioned styles of authoritarianism and censorship, the lack of a critical culture, and a poverty of resources. What I would like to suggest, though, is that criticism is flourishing everywhere and that our task is not to deny this but to identify, channel and amplify its manifold messages.

The appearance – the look – of buildings is at once both the least and the most interesting thing about them. The least, if it is the hinge by which architecture is reduced to sculpture, to a 'pure' form described in private languages: something self-referential, hermetic, detached and canonical. The most, though, if it offers an opening to architecture's multiple possibilities for representation, its rich and shifting dialectic of form and content. This ultimate resistance to abstraction – this intrinsic multiplicity of meanings – results from architecture's literal inhabitation and is what distinguishes it from other artistic expressions. The social is not the *context* of architecture but its substance. And this is the reason why everybody can – and does – read it, from the most effete theoretician to the infant crawling across the cold floor towards the warming rug.

Architecture's own polyvalence should also remind us that its critical tradition is highly diverse, that the codification of the architect's responsibilities by the Babylonian king Hammurabi in the eighteenth century BC is as consequential as the dismay expressed about the nineteenth-century in-dustrial city by architect A. W. Pugin, or the defence of contemporary neighbourhood ecologies by the late great urbanist Jane Jacobs. This interweaving of architecture with the social life that pro-duces it and that it, in turn, supports has produced the formal tradition of architectural commen-tary and critique, which dates back millennia, and assures us that it has always come from multi-ple perspectives and has been embodied in multiple discourses. The task of criticism is surely not to 'resolve' this polyphony in a single approach (like the fine arts style dominant today), but to en-able more voices to be heard.

We all come from countries in which architectural activities are conducted under the framework of building codes, planning ordinances, and other legal instruments that define – sometimes with overwhelming specificity – an idea about 'good' architecture. Setting aside, for a moment, ques-tions of the legal manipulation of matters of appearance – requirements to design in historical or 'contextual' fashion or to include a portrait of the President, Dear Leader, Dictator, or Sheikh in the lobby –, it is clear that both the utility and forms of our buildings and cities have been dramat-ically influenced by the legal frameworks that site, organise and judge them, frameworks that – how-ever fraudulently – rest their authority on an idea of social benefit.

Contemporary architecture is very much the product of a series of innovations that were conceptu-alised performatively and only later worked out morphologically. Demands originating in move-ments for social transformation and equity were translated into laws requiring day-lighting, venti-lation, heating, sanitation and protection from fire. We know something about the disastrous con-sequences of the *evasion* of seismic regulations in Japan and Turkey, and it is the general recognition of the importance of those standards that makes flaunting them so scandalous. Only because of the existence of an enormous body of criticism – some of it from the community of architecture – are we able to take the necessity of these fundamental qualities of our building for granted: its essential imbrication with an idea of the common good.

Today, we are passing through a period in which the shape of buildings and cities is in desperate need of reconfiguration, a continuation of the historic process of re-describing architecture in terms of both how it must act and how it must be: what its fundamental qualities are. Just as many of the reforms that established the parameters of building today are the direct outcome of specific disasters – fires, earthquakes, cyclones and epidemics –, radical transformations in architecture (for both good and ill) are being produced by more contemporary crises, by situations that are the logical fo-cus for the work of architectural criticism, a practice in which some form of advocacy must always be embedded.

The first of these crises falls under the rubric of 'the environment' and will inevitably alter virtually every aspect of the way in which we design. The acceleration of climate change is very real, and our buildings, cities and transportation infrastructure are directly implicated. Although the United States is the disproportionate champion in producing greenhouse gasses, consuming energy from non-renewable sources and setting an unsustainable model for overdevelopment, it is joined by the rest of the world in increasing degree. China currently has a level of car ownership comparable to that in the United States in 1912 and seems determined to match our ridiculous over-dependence on the automobile. Recent studies of air quality in India – the first such to be undertaken comprehensively – reveal levels of pollution that frequently exceed recognised standards of safety by truly appalling amounts. The Gulf region is engaged in a frenzied building boom anchored literally and figuratively in petroleum. If there is an apt symbol of the global energy potlatch now underway – and the enduring association of status and waste – it is surely the huge indoor ski-slope in a shopping mall in Dubai, soon to be topped by an even larger version under construction down the road.

The situation of a warming, toxic, degraded, planetary environment – and an exponentially growing population now topping six billion – has fundamental consequences for architecture and for the culture we collaborate in producing that defines both its character and reception. While it is surely the duty of critics to hold the line for architectural quality – to celebrate the artistic achievements of contemporary architects such as Rem Koolhaas, Zaha Hadid, or Frank Gehry, and to explain expressive nuances and systems of meaning –, we are mistaken if we think that the territory of formal analysis can simply be isolated from other concerns, protected by the mantle of 'free expression', or by the notion that all artistic works engage the world at comparable distance. A poem written in the nineteenth century by Emily Dickinson on the back of a scrap of paper and relegated to a drawer is a very different affair than a gigantic sealed glass building in the desert or a huge titanium flower in Spain. Not to contravene the First Law of Thermodynamics, but there is no question that, in our sphere, energy can be lost. Virtually no material embodies more energy than titanium. And the BTUs blown cooling Dubai or Vegas might clean all the drinking water of Africa.

It may be that the duty of architectural critics nowadays is less to rise in defence of 'architecture' than to defend the planet from too much of it. Our tasks are immediately different from those confronted by Clement Greenberg, Anthony Blunt, and other art critics of less hybrid forms of expression. Because every work of architecture maps a set of social relations, because every work of architecture accounts for a complex of distributive decisions about global resources, and because every work of architecture colludes in the literal creation of the world climate, criticism cannot escape taking these matters into account. However hard it may attempt to retreat behind the veil of 'objectivity', criticism is always a form of propaganda, precisely because these inescapable dimensions of architecture ineluctably render its judgements political. The duty of the critic, therefore, is both to consider the larger meanings of his or her preoccupations or circumspections and to empower his or her readers with an analytical tool with which to make the environment more comprehensible and tractable, to make the *public* more critical. To be sure, this can mean — as it did in the debates that originated the era of post-modernity — a fight to defend the aesthetic basis of architecture, to protect it from vulgar theories of reflexive instrumentality: a work of architecture is always also a work of art.

This political aspect of criticism is engaged directly by the dire condition of the environment and architecture's role in creating this condition or curing it. Given architecture's fundamentally conservative position at the end of a chain of decisions and as the product of the concentration of fiscal and material resources, the task of critics — like that of those social reformers who had such a strong impact on building practices in the nineteenth and twentieth centuries — is to fight for the renewal of the legal and conceptual frameworks of building to make sustainability as uncontroversial an element in architectural culture as sanitary plumbing, fire-safety, or seismic protection. This is a model that demands action before fact, not simply the canny analysis of the object once standing. But it also means that the nature of connoisseurship — instead of being an arcane, distancing, elitist practice — must be enriched by additional categories of expertise and judgement, that we must empower ourselves to both lovingly describe the lush patina of oxidising COR-TEN™ and elegant systems for the passive extraction of hot air.

This form-follows-disaster model also becomes widely influential in the wake of quicker moving natural disasters, including the South Asian tsunami of December 2004 and Hurricane Katrina of August 2005. Katrina was both a remarkably terrible and remarkably clarifying event. Like the tsunami, it called into question large-scale patterns of settlement, including the logic of building (and rebuilding) on endangered coastlines, the destruction of natural wetlands, barrier islands and other forms of natural protection, even the viability of one of the United States' most important cities, New Orleans. It has also resulted in dramatic debates about logical building typologies and construction methods, and has, with blistering impact, revealed the deep distributive inequities that underlie all those patterns. If ever architectural criticism were offered a synthetic, focal moment, this was it: the conjunction of environmental, social, structural, economic and expressive issues was a 'perfect storm'. It was also one of those moments at which the task of criticism was widely dispersed, an event that obliged almost every observer to formulate opinions on core questions of architecture and urbanism.

Katrina showed that there is both a very widespread common language for the discussion of architecture, and that its deployment is instantaneous in demanding circumstances. Could it be that the complaint by many critics in these pages about their marginalisation expresses the pain of a self-inflicted wound? Could there possibly be greater public interest in debating the form of the city, the role of architecture, the laying out of infrastructure, the meaning of community, than there has been in the wake of Katrina? Architects have scarcely been parsimonious with suggestions and their contending variety has provided a smorgasbord of setups for critical intervention. And these are the times and places where our intervention is important, where lives – not brands – are at stake.

Disasters *are* criticism because they force reflection on their origins and interrogate the structure of life – both social and physical – that we are accustomed to thinking of as normal. One sometimes uses the phrase "a disaster waiting to happen" to describe a situation that is susceptible to a known form of trouble: an un-reinforced building in an active seismic zone, a 'fire trap', or a slum of injurious, fomenting injustice and discontent. Clearly, such sites demand the work of criticism and give it purpose: critics can be the canaries in the coal mine. But it is misleading to suggest that architecture has an invariably positivist trajectory, that the cycle of challenge and reform repeats itself uniformly as outcome. Critics must distinguish disasters of our own creation and identify developments which, in the guise of reform or 'safety', are actually regressive, perpetuating rather than ameliorating our jeopardy.

These un-natural disasters form an urgent substrate for all of us, and architecture must be discussed both in its role as accessory and as the ledger in which these circumstances are recorded. No more stark instance of this exists than the exponential growth of slums. Half the world population now lives in cities, and of these half live in slums. It is not possible that the architecture of hundreds of millions of people should be outside our purview, that we should reserve our focus on the historic cores of unsustainable megacities, or myopically cheer the fevered growth of their gigantic, perpetually inadequate infrastructures and their generic architectures and environments. We must not confirm these deadly patterns, whether through enthusiasm or indifference, or by confining our practices simply to projects that fall within conventional notions of 'quality'. Architecture is – and records – a living condition; our choice of focus will either defend or subvert ideas of freedom, equity and difference.

Writing this as the airwaves are again dominated by images of destruction in the Middle East, another deeply influential set of disasters of our own making leaps to the foreground. There is an old joke about military music being a perfect oxymoron. Unfortunately, military architecture is no such thing, and the history of architecture and urbanism is inextricably interwoven with the exigencies of warfare, a connection that seems only to deepen of late. Our 'father' Vitruvius devoted a major portion of his treatise to the arts of fortification, and the Roman *imperium* spread its colonising tentacles via cities that elaborated the gridded order of military camps. Until very recent times, cities were literally surrounded by walls, and defensive measures certainly might have been part of the Neanderthal schmooze at that primal campfire.

We continue to live with the consequences of our own violence. During the Cold War years, both America and China pursued policies of dramatic de-urbanisation as a defence against the atomic war, and even the neutral Swiss — who have the resources to put behind their anxiety — legislated a bomb-shelter in every basement. As ever, civic investment in guns shortchanged butter and deformed the idea of public culture, the site where an architecture of life most urgently needs to flourish. Make no mistake: this is a zero sum game. Every base and bunker built means one fewer library, school, sewer, housing block, or clinic. As a hundred die every day in Iraq, as bombs blast Beirut and Gaza, as rockets rain on Haifa, the images of shattered bodies and buildings scream that our addiction to violence must be controlled for architecture itself to live. Isn't it our task to help banish forever this evil branch of the family, the one that builds Security Fences, Pentagons, pillboxes, refugee camps, Kalashnikov-stuffed caves, and the rest of the infrastructure of violent death?

The 9/11 attack galvanised a discussion of architecture and planning that was nearly universal in New York. This was the direst physical disaster the city — which has been spared the direct effects of war since the days of the Revolution — has ever faced. As a result, New York and other American cities are now decking themselves out with a huge defensive apparatus that is transforming both the cityscape and the way in which we inhabit it. Thousands of bollards and anti-bomb planters litter the streets. The building code is undergoing another revision to better prepare structures to withstand attack. Although much of this is sensible from the standpoint of 'normal' emergencies — more secure escape stairs are important in a fire, whatever its origins —, much of it reflects a manipulated paranoia that only serves the end of a contracted and manipulated public realm. The slow progress of rebuilding at Ground Zero has been an endless object lesson in the relationship of architecture and power and in the way in which the public meanings of building are established and controlled.

Architecture's highly ambiguous role in all of this has provided endless opportunities for critical reflection, and — in this most media-saturated environment on earth — the discussion has been brisk if ultimately ineffectual in influencing an outcome that has been, for the most part, decided outside the democratic arena. However, the use of 9/11 to produce the vast new apparatus of Homeland Security — and to manufacture consent to it — has also provided a bridge for architectural criticism to enter one of the most challenging realms it currently confronts: the importance of virtual space and its arrangements to any serious contemplation of the built environment. While it is still possible to sustain a degree of enthusiasm for the liberatory possibilities of the electronic 'global village', it is also clear that the conjunction of new technology with state and corporate power has had dramatically different consequences.

Those bollards and blast-proof lobbies are the visible tip of a giant iceberg of surveillance and manipulation that has fundamental implications for our relationship to space, affecting the nature of our 'right to the city', our privacy, our ease of movement, and our freedom of association and assembly. These are core issues for architecture, and they are being challenged from all sides, whether by suicide bombers, police departments, or multinational hucksters. These forces see architecture militarily, a phenomenon that either complies with and advances their agendas, or an obstacle to be destroyed, whether literally or by being made transparent to their panoptic gaze. Architectural criticism must find a way to confront both what it can and cannot see, and to recognise that its own situation has been radically changed, and will become even more marginalised if it insists on being no more than the instrument of intellectual and spatial nostalgia.

If the magnitude of the 9/11 tragedy exceeded all others, the response has been in many ways familiar. New York's great debates about its future have often followed focal events. The Triangle Shirtwaist fire of 1911, in which 146 garment workers – mainly young women – died because they could not escape, led directly to improved regulations for building safety. The construction of the Equitable Insurance Company building in 1915 – an early skyscraper that rose 165 metres straight up from the street – galvanised the rapid passage of New York's pioneering 1916 bulk-zoning laws that invented the 'classic' stepping profiles (designed to bring daylight to the public street) that characterised our buildings until the dopey, modernist-inspired revisions of the 1960s. The 1963 demolition of the much-loved Pennsylvania Station (designed by McKim, Meade, and White in 1910 after the model of the third-century Baths of Caracalla in Rome) was a defining moment in the birth of the preservation movement that has been so crucial – in good ways and bad – to ideas about the relationship of stability and change in a city that was suddenly forced to confront its own historic character.

If I seem to return over and over to the confrontational role of criticism, it is because criticism itself can arise only in situations in which there are alternatives. Criticism defines a position within a context in which others are also possible, and uses its tools argumentatively, to demonstrate the logic and consequences of a point of view. Architectural criticism is rhetorical in its obligation to persuade, and political in its obligation to the social, to the distinguishing dimension of architecture. In choosing the location of an argument, the critic selectively distorts, looking for sites of opportunity to persuasively reveal the results of his or her experience and analysis. In a society governed entirely by 'tradition', there can be no criticism because of the presumption that everything has already been consented to (or in which the very idea of consent is foreign), and that the only task of the intellect is transmission or reproduction: the paradigm is fixed. Once, however, the idea of the plural is broached, criticism becomes both necessary and inevitable.

Debates about the importance of traditional architectures (and Modernism now takes its place among them) – whether focused on the authenticity of style, on prescriptive social morphology, or on the importance of *l'art pour l'art* – arise only in the context of challenge, of the availability of other ways of seeing and doing. If there has been a general drift in critical theory over the past thirty years or so (however 'Western' one might elect to see this phenomenon), it has been to question the idea of the absolute: the notion that 'truth' is stable and universal. While there are many who question the implications of such 'relativistic' reasoning and the dangers it poses in particular to the ethical dimension of life, it nonetheless seems clear that the world *is* radically diverse and that even common objectives can be approached from many directions. The reality of difference also means that the importance of tradition – however this is understood – must be argued in ways that are comprehensible to those who stand outside it. A critic cannot simply assert the timelessness of any given traditional architecture, but must connect it to its role in culture, its ability to fulfill a building's obligation to the environment, its importance as an element in humanity's mosaic of achievement, its ability to conduce the happiness of its inhabitants, or – to address the ethical obligations of the other more directly – must invoke the importance of tolerance for another's free choices.

Such choices about architecture are made a billion times a day, and each of these depends on some mechanism of distinction. Whether it is the bank that 'redlines' a poor neighbourhood for disinvestment, the suburbanite selecting wallpaper at the Home Depot, the board of trustees at a museum hiring a star architect in hopes of attracting crowds, the bomber pilot 'illuminating' a building for destruction, the developer looking for a cheap patch of land, the preservationist defending a historic church, or the favela-dweller sorting through a scrap pile looking for something with which to patch his roof, the built environment is not an unconscious product but a compilation of choices based on an infinite repertoire of criteria. Architectural criticism, as a discipline, can only operate in the context of this bloom of preferences, contingencies and demands.

To find our own ways through this thicket of determinacies, however, we must formulate criteria that we must then constantly hone and test. There are four ideas that we should all bear in mind. The first is that architecture is always instrumental. Building alters the way people live, the way the planet is configured, the availability of resources, and the way space and its memory are organised. Architecture is not an abstraction, but a concrete proposition about human activity. In analysing architecture, this means – a second point – that we should never understand our task as standing above the quantitative. The relevance of architectural criticism is founded in its cognisance of the measurable, one of the origin points of architecture itself. Building exists in a social, ecological and gravitational environment, and can and must be weighed on the scales of survival and equity. We cannot ignore the resources buildings consume, the environmental and social effects of their operation, and their adequacy to people's material needs.

Third, architectural criticism must never lose sight of the artistic dimension of its object while remembering all the while that architecture's aesthetic expression is uniquely contingent. This does not disqualify any system of meaning, however arcane. It does insist, though, that it accounts for its compatibilities with the other systems of signification that architecture invariably contains. This relationship can be critical – even antagonistic – but it cannot be, by definition, absent. And finally, architectural criticism is obliged to support the primary duty of architecture itself: making life better. This is the lamp that should illumine every building we make and every sentence we write.

Appendix

LIST OF AUTHORS IN THIS MONOGRAPH
AND SEMINAR PARTICIPANTS

IBRAHIM ABA AL-KHAIL
Architect; publisher and Editor in Chief, *Albenaa*, Saudi Arabia.

KAMRAN ADLE
Photographer; Editor, *Iranian Journal of Architecture*.

KAMRAN AFSHAR NADERI
Architect; architectural critic, *Memar*, Iran.

OMAR AKBAR
Architect; Director, Bauhaus Dessau Foundation, Germany; member, 2007 Aga Khan Award for Architecture Steering Committee.

NADER ARDALAN
Architect; Senior Vice President of Design, KEO International Consultants, Kuwait / Qatar / United Arab Emirates / Lebanon; Fellow, Center for Middle Eastern Studies, Harvard University, United States.

MOHAMMAD AL-ASAD
Architect and architectural historian; Chairman of the Board of Directors and Senior Advisor, Center for the Study of the Built Environment, Jordan.

AYDAN BALAMIR
Architect and educator; Associate Professor, Faculty of Architecture, Middle East Technical University, Turkey.

TREVOR BODDY
Architectural critic, curator, historian, educator and urban designer, Canada.

STEFANO BOERI
Architect and urban planner; Editor, *Domus*, Italy.

OLE BOUMAN
Designer and cultural historian; Editor, *Volume*, The Netherlands.

ALI CENGIZKAN
Architect and poet; Associate Professor, Faculty of Architecture, Middle East Technical University, Turkey; Editor, *Middle East Technical University Journal of the Faculty of Architecture*, Turkey.

FRANÇOIS CHASLIN
Architectural critic, France.

MANUEL CUADRA
Critic and educator; Director, International Committee of Architectural Critics (CICA), Germany.

HUSSAIN MOUSA DASHTI
Architect and educator; Assistant Professor, Department of Architecture, Kuwait University, Kuwait.

PETER DAVEY
Architectural critic; former Editor, *The Architectural Review*, United Kingdom.

FARROKH DERAKHSHANI
Architect; Director, Aga Khan Award for Architecture, Switzerland.

DARAB DIBA
Architect and educator; Editor, *Memari va Shahrsazi*, Iran; Professor of Architecture, Tehran University, Iran.

OSAMA AL-DUAIJ
Architect; Managing Director, Engineering Systems Group, Kuwait; President, Advanced Systems Group, Kuwait; President, Organising Committee, 1st Arab Architecture/Design Expo; member, Organising Committee, Middle East Architecture Forum.

INGEBORG FLAGGE
Architect and educator; former Director, Deutsches Architektur Museum, Germany.

LUIS FERNÁNDEZ-GALIANO
Architectural critic; Editor, *Arquitectura Viva* and *El País*, Spain; Professor, Universidad Politécnica de Madrid, Spain.

JORGE GLUSBERG
Art and architectural critic; Director, Centro de Arte Y Communicacion, Argentina.

LOUISE NOELLE GRAS
Architectural critic; co-founder and Director, International Committee of Architectural Critics (CICA), Mexico; researcher, Institute of Aesthetic Studies, National University of Mexico, Mexico.

DOĞAN HASOL
Architect and author; Editor, *Yapi*, Turkey.

RENATA HOLOD
Architectural historian; Professor, Department of History of Art; Curator, Near East Section, University Museum; Director, Program for Visual Studies; President-Elect of Historians of Islamic Art Association (HIAA); University of Pennsylvania, United States.

LLUIS HORTET
Lawyer; Director, Mies van der Rohe Foundation, Spain.

MOHAMED A. IBRAHIM
Architect and educator; Chairman, Centre for Planning and Architectural Studies, Egypt.

ROBERT IVY
Architectural critic; Editor in Chief, *Architectural Record*, United States; Vice President and Editorial Director, McGraw-Hill Construction Media, United States.

SALLY KHANAFER, AFNAN AL RABAIAN
and AYESHA AL SAGER
Newly-graduating architects, Kuwait University, Kuwait.

ROMI KHOSLA
Architect, India.

ADEL AL-KHURAFI
Engineer; Managing Director, Kuwait Pipe Industries and Oil Services Company; Chairman, Kuwait Society of Engineers.

MOUHSEN MAKSOUD
Architect; Editor in Chief, *Ibda'at Handasiyya*, Syria.

ROWAN MOORE
Architectural critic; Director, The Architecture Foundation, United Kingdom.

MAJD MUSA
Architect and researcher; advisor and former Documentation Program Manager, Center for the Study of the Built Environment, Jordan; Ph.D. candidate in Architecture, University of Illinois at Urbana-Champaign, United States.

MASHARY A. AL-NAIM
Architect, author and educator; Senior Editor, *Albenaa*, Saudi Arabia; Associate Professor, College of Architecture and Planning, King Faisal University, Saudi Arabia.

SUHA ÖZKAN
Architectural theoretician and educator; Chairman, World Architecture Community; former Secretary General, Aga Khan Award for Architecture.

SUNEET PAUL
Author; Managing Editor, *Architecture + Design (a+d)* and *Indian Design and Interiors (IDI)*, India.

SAM PICKENS
Information Officer, Aga Khan Development Network, Switzerland.

JEAN-MICHEL PLACE
Publisher, *L'Architecture d'Aujourd'hui* and *Techniques et Architecture*, France.

JASSIM M. QABAZARD
Engineer; President, JQEC/Jassim Qabazard Engineering Consultants; Deputy Chairman, Kuwait Society of Engineers; Deputy Chairman, JQE Consultants, Kuwait.

HANI RASHID
Architect; Principal, Asymptote, United States; member, 2007 Aga Khan Award for Architecture Steering Committee.

JOSEPH RYKWERT
Architectural historian; Paul Philippe Cret Professor of Architecture and Professor of Art History, Emeritus, Department of Architecture, University of Pennsylvania, United States; President, International Committee of Architectural Critics (CICA), United Kingdom.

MODJTABA SADRIA
Philosopher; Professor, Cross-Cultural Relations and East Asian Studies, Chuo University, Japan; member, 2007 Aga Khan Award for Architecture Steering Committee.

LUAY AHMAD AL-SALEH
Principal, Luay Ahmad Al-Saleh Architectural Consultants; Chairman, Kuwait League of Architects.

DINA SATTAROVA
Author; Editor in Chief, *Dizain i Novaia Arhitectura*, Tatarstan, Russian Federation; General Director, Architecture Development Fund, Russian Federation.

YASMIN SHARIFF
Architect; partner, Dennis Sharp Architects, United Kingdom; Senior Lecturer, Department of Architecture, University of Westminster, United Kingdom.

DENNIS SHARP
Architect, author and editor; partner, Dennis Sharp Architects, United Kingdom; Editor, *International Architecture*; former Editor, *AA Quarterly* and *World Architecture*, United Kingdom; Chairman, International Committee of Architectural Critics (CICA), United Kingdom.

MURTUZA SHIKOH
Architect; Editor, *Archi Times* and *Architecture + Interiors (A + I)*, Pakistan.

MICHAEL SORKIN
Architect, architectural critic, author and educator; Principal, Michael Sorkin Studio, United States; Director, Graduate Urban Design Program, The City College of New York (CCNY), United States; Contributing Editor, *Architectural Record*, *Metropolis* and *ID Magazine*, United States.

BUDI A. SUKADA
Architect and architectural critic; President, Indonesian Institute of Architects; Editor, *IAI Journal*, Indonesia.

TIMUR TUREKULOV
Architect; Director and Editor in Chief, *Kumbez*, Kazakhstan.

Acknowledgments

Architectural Criticism and Journalism was the topic of a seminar organised by the Aga Khan Award for Architecture and sponsored by the Kuwait Society of Engineers (KSE) on 6 and 7 December 2005 in Kuwait City. The seminar was organised in collaboration with the International Committee of Architectural Critics (CICA) and the Kuwait League of Architects. The international seminar was the final component of the *Middle East Architecture and Design Conference and Exhibition*, a week-long event organised by KSE and inaugurated by His Highness Sheikh Sabah al-Ahmad al-Sabah, who was then Prime Minister of Kuwait.

Since 1978, the Aga Khan Award has conducted over twenty-one international and regional seminars. Plans for the seminar in Kuwait were initiated by Mr Osama Al-Duaij, who, together with KSE and under the able leadership of its chairman, Mr Adel Al-Khurafi, efficiently organised this Award event. The voluntary efforts of over one hundred members of KSE ensured the success of the conference and exhibition, as well as the seminar, and Mr Al-Khurafi's staff and colleagues at KSE provided invaluable support for all aspects of the event. I would also like to extend my special thanks to Ms Nargues Adle, who very capably coordinated the participation of the Award's international guests. At the Award Office in Geneva, Mrs Karen Stylianoudis was instrumental in organising the seminar, as well as Ms Anne-Hélène Decaux, who provided assistance in Kuwait.

The seminar programme was developed with Professor Dennis Sharp, Chairman of CICA.

The seminar proceedings were prepared by a team from the Center for the Study of the Built Environment (CSBE) in Amman, Jordan. The editor is Dr Mohammad al-Asad, who founded CSBE and was its director until recently; he is currently a senior advisor and chairman of the centre's Board of Directors. The associate editor is Ms Majd Musa, who managed CSBE's documentation programme and has recently moved on to pursue a doctorate in architecture. Editorial and proofreading support was provided by Ms Sandra Hiari, research and coordination officer at CSBE. In addition, Ms Jumanah Akrouk, adjunct editor at CSBE, carried out the initial review and sorting of the essays featured in the proceedings.

The portfolio of colour images, including the cover photographs, is all by Mr Kamran Adle. The illustrations on pages 55–58, 77–81 and 164–168 have been provided by the authors of the essays.

I would also like to thank Mr Umberto Allemandi, chairman, and all of his staff and colleagues at Umberto Allemandi & C. in Turin for their efforts in realising this publication. In particular, Ms Harriet Graham coordinated the publication and undertook all of the copy-editing, and Ms Nicole Kerr-Munslow and Mr Rosario Pavia provided valuable support in bringing the publication to fruition.

FARROKH DERAKHSHANI
Director, Aga Khan Award for Architecture

www.akdn.org

EDITORIAL COORDINATION FARROKH DERAKHSHANI (FOR AKTC); HARRIET GRAHAM (FOR UMBERTO ALLEMANDI & C.)

EDITORIAL SUPPORT SANDRA HIARI (FOR CSBE)

COPY-EDITING HARRIET GRAHAM

LAYOUT ROSARIO PAVIA

PHOTOLITHOGRAPHY FOTOMEC, TURIN, ITALY

PUBLISHED BY UMBERTO ALLEMANDI & C., TURIN, ITALY

PRINTED IN ITALY, DECEMBER 2006

ISBN 88-422-1480-9